Primarily Plants

A PLANT STUDY FOR K-3

Editors

JUDITH HILLEN
AIMS Education Foundation
Fresno Pacific College

EVALYN HOOVER
AIMS Education Foundation
Fresno Unified School District

Principal Authors

EVALYN HOOVER
Science Specialist
Fresno Unified School District

SHERYL MERCIER
Science/Health Coordinator
Fresno Unified School District

Illustrator

Sheryl Mercier

Contributing Author

Dinah Brown

This book contains materials developed by the AIMS Education Foundation in cooperation with the Fresno Unified School District. **AIMS** (**A**ctivities **I**ntegrating **M**athematics and **S**cience) began in 1981 with a grant from the National Science Foundation. The non-profit AIMS Education Foundation publishes hands-on instructional materials (books and the monthly AIMS Newsletter) that integrate curricular disciplines such as mathematics, science, language arts, and social studies. The Foundation sponsors a national program of professional development through which educators may gain both an understanding of the AIMS philosophy and expertise in teaching by integrated, hands-on methods.

ISBN 1-881431-24-X

Printed in the United States of America

TABLE OF CONTENTS

Special Thanks

to

Fresno Unified Science Specialists

Care Butler
Evalyn Hoover
Sharon Kinnear
Howard Larimer
Sheryl Mercier
Betsy Olson
Hal Silvani
Jeri Starkweather
Peter Summers
Mike Walsh

The writers also wish to thank
the many classroom teachers in Fresno Unified
who willingly shared many creative ideas.

I HEAR, AND I FORGET

I SEE, AND I REMEMBER

I DO, AND I UNDERSTAND

–Chinese Proverb

Why Study Plants?

Plants are extremely important to life on earth. They grow in almost every part of the world - on moutain tops, in the ocean, and in many desert and polar regions. Without plants, there could be no life on earth. The oxygen in the air is produced by plants and the food we eat comes from plants or animals that eat plants.

Plants supply people with food, clothing, and shelter. Many of our most useful medicines are made from plants. Plants also provide us with beauty and pleasure.

Plants are probably most important to people as food. We eat seeds of plants as corn, rice, and wheat. When we eat carrots or beets, we are eating the roots of plants. We eat stems of asparagus and celery plants, the leaves of lettuce and cabbage plants, the flowers of broccoli and cauliflower plants, and the fruits of apples, bananas and orange trees.

Important raw materials come from plants. Trees give us lumber and other products. Cotton fiber is used for fabrics and clothing. Hemp is used to make rope.

Plants also provide an important source of fuel. People all over the world use wood to heat their homes or cook their food. Three sources of our fuel - coal, oil, and natural gas - all come from plants that lived long ago.

A number of medicines come from plants. Quinine, used for treating malaria, comes from the bark of the cinchona tree. Penicillin comes from tiny plants called fungi. Yeast, a fungus, is used to produce alcohol and to make bread "rise".

CALIFORNIA STATE SCIENCE FRAMEWORK*

Science Framework Concept: Biological Science—Plants K-3

- Most plants grow in soil.
- All plants need water.
- Growth and reproduction of plants are affected by temperature.
- Plants do not tolerate extremes in temperature.
- Green plants need light.
- Many kinds of green plants have roots, stems, leaves, and flowers.
- Flowers produce seed that grows into new plants.
- Ferns and mosses are simple green plants.
- Plants can be grown for use and enjoyment.
- Soils provide the water and minerals that plants need.
- Roots anchor plants and absorb minerals and water from the soil.
- Stems support plants and transport their fluids.
- Leaves absorb sunlight and produce the plant's food.
- Seeds require certain conditions such as proper temperature and moisture, in order to germinate.
- Some flowering plants can reproduce asexually from vegetative parts such as roots and stems.

*Reference: With regard to the Big Ideas of the proposed 1990 California State Science Framework, the lessons and experiences presented here correlate well with themes of Stability, Patterns of Change, Energy, Evolution, Systems and Interactions, and Scale and Structure.

MATERIALS

NON-CONSUMABLE ITEMS

_______ aluminum foil
_______ Ziplock type baggies
_______ transparent tape or double sided tape
_______ magnifying lens
_______ clear plastic cups
_______ small Dixie cups
_______ sharp knife
_______ heater (optional)
_______ ice chest (optional)
_______ paper bags
_______ balance scales
_______ centimeter tape
_______ plastic bags
_______ paper towels
_______ paper plates
_______ box
_______ flower pots or plastic containers
_______ crayons

CONSUMABLE ITEMS

_______ beans—lima, broad, kidney, garbanzo
_______ seeds—corn, sunflower, popcorn, blackeyed peas, radish
_______ bulbs—onions, garlic, daffodils, tulips, narcissus
_______ soils—potting, sand, clay, schoolyard dirt
_______ fresh fruits and vegetables—oranges, apples, lemons, bell peppers, melons, tomatoes, peas, avocados, peaches, carrots, beets, radishes, sweet potatoes
_______ fern fronds
_______ house plants
_______ milk cartons (from school lunches)
_______ ice
_______ maple sugar
_______ cotton cloth
_______ cotton and corn plants
_______ food coloring
_______ butcher paper
_______ vegetable stems—celery, potatoes, asparagus
_______ flowers—daisies
_______ leaves
_______ contact paper
_______ seeds—wind blown (dandelion, milkweed, maple, sycamore, pine)
—water carried (cranberry, coconut)
—hitchhikers (cocklebur, crabgrass, beggar ticks, thistle)

Plant Growth

Plants are organisms that grow and reproduce their own kind. They must have food, air, water, sunlight, and space in order to grow.

Green plants produce food and oxygen from water, carbon dioxide, and minerals through a process called photosynthesis. They take in carbon dioxide from the air, water and minerals from the soil, and energy from the sunlight. During photosynthesis, carbon dioxide and water are united in the presence of chlorophyll to form sugar and oxygen. Some of the food produced by a green plant is used by the plant as it grows and produces leaves and fruit. The remaining food is converted to starch and stored in the plant.

Scientists have identified more than 350,000 kinds of plants. They fall into two basic categories - flowering and non-flowering plants. Those that produce flowers grow from seeds while nonflowering plants such as ferns, mosses, molds, and mildew grow from spores.

Flowering plants grow from seeds. A sprouting seed must absorb water before it will start to grow. It must also have soil firmly packed around it and warmth from the sun. Inside the seed is a tiny embryo, surrounded by stored food. When the embryo starts growing, roots grow downward and a stem grows upward. Once the stem breaks through the surface of the soil into the sunlight, the first two true leaves form and the plant begins to make food. When plants have water, sunlight, and the proper minerals in the soil, they grow, manufacture food, and give off oxygen.

Nonflowering plants grow from spores. Like a seed, a spore develops into an embryo. Unlike a seed, the spore does not contain food for the embryo to grow. The plant that develops, must get food elsewhere.

Inside a Seed

I. Topic Area
Biological Science: Plants—Seeds

II. Introductory Statement
Students will observe lima beans that have been soaked in water overnight and identify the major parts of the seed.

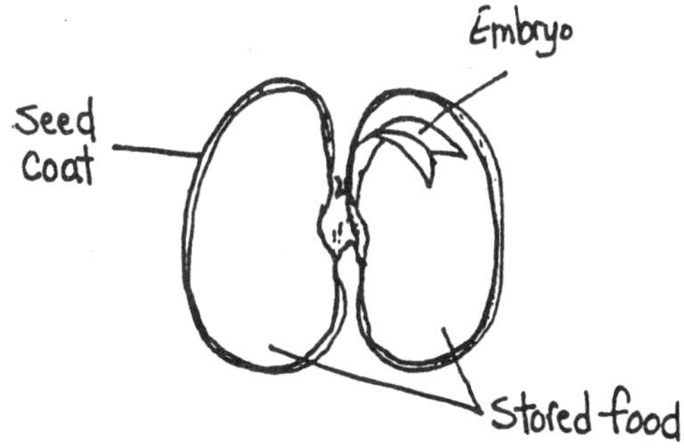

III. Math Skills
a. Measurement

Science Processes
a. Observing
b. Comparing
c. Recording Data

IV. Materials
Large lima beans or other broad beans

V. Key Question
How can we look inside a seed to see how a plant begins?

VI. Background Information
All seeds consist of two parts, the little plant or embryo and the seed coat. The seed coat protects the developing plant; the embryo is inside the seed. Cotyledons store food. They are the leaves that are attached to the little plant or embryo. When the seed begins to grow, one part of the embryo becomes the root and the rest becomes the upper stem and leaves.

VII. Management Suggestions
Large lima bean seeds are easy to handle. Soak the beans overnight so the seed coats are loose and easy to handle.

VIII. Procedure
1. Distribute one water soaked seed and one dry lima bean seed to each student.
2. Observe and describe the dry seed. Describe it in terms of color, texture, firmness, etc. Trace the seed on the ruler and measure its length.
3. How is the wet seed different from the dry seed?
4. Look at the seed coat and find the spot where the seed was attached to the pod. This small hole in the seed coat lets water into the seed. Carefully remove the seed coat and place it to one side. Identify on the worksheet.
5. Carefully split the seed into two parts. Look at the two halves. Identify the embryo. Find the food storage area of the plant.

IX. Discussion
1. What did the dry seed look like? Was the skin wrinkled? Could you find the spot where the seed was attached to the pod? What did it look like?
2. After the seed was soaked, what happened to it? What did the skin you removed look like?
3. Describe the insides of a seed. Can you find the embryo? What does it look like? Can you see the shape of the future leaves?
4. Does the food storage area look the same in all seeds?
5. Do all seeds look alike when split open? Why or why not?

X. Extensions
1. Use red beans to compare with the lima beans.
2. Try other large dicot seeds to see how they compare with the lima bean seed.
3. Open peanuts (roasted or plain). Observe the embryo inside the bean, then eat the evidence.

Inside a Seed

Scientist: ____________________

1. What does the dry seed look like? ____________________

____

2. How big is the dry seed? Trace the seed on the ruler.

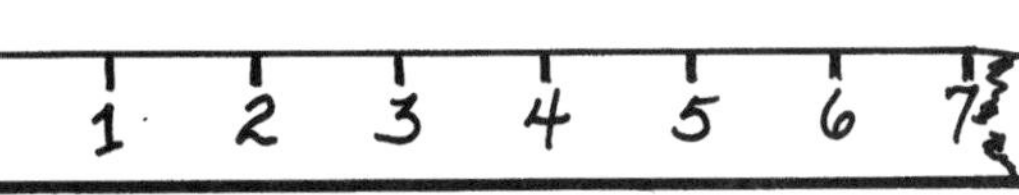

3. Soak the dry seed in water overnight.

How is the wet seed different from a dry seed?

____

____

4. Split the seed in half. What does it look like on the inside? Look for the tiny plant called the embryo.

____

____

5. Why do you think there is so much food stored for the tiny plant (embryo)?

____

Inside a Seed

_______________ Scientist

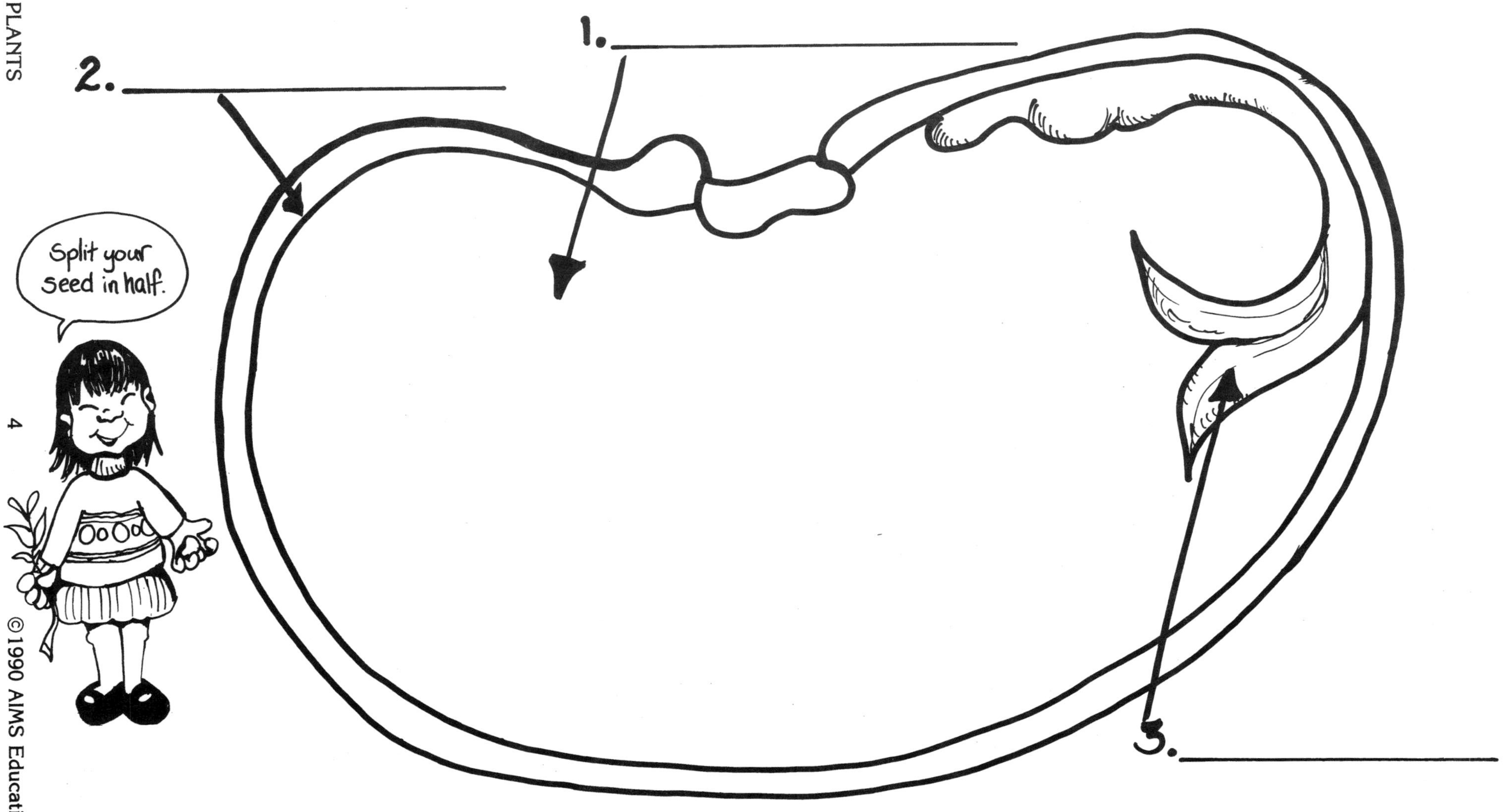

1. _______________

2. _______________

3. _______________

Split your seed in half.

Label the parts: food storage, seed coat, little plant (embryo).

A Seed Grows

I. Topic Area
Biological Science: Plants—Seeds become plants

II. Introductory Statement
Students will grow a bean seed and watch how a plant begins.

III. Math Skills
a. Predicting
b. Measuring
c. Graphing

Science Processes
a. Observing
b. Comparing
c. Recording Data

IV. Materials
Lima beans
Ziplock type baggies
Paper towels

V. Key Question
How does a seed grow?

VI. Background Information

Seeds start to grow when conditions are right to support the needs of growing plants. Water, air and proper temperature are all necessary for seed growth. Water makes the seed swell and softens the seed coat. The embryo begins to grow. A warm temperature is also needed for a seed to germinate. Many seeds begin to grow in the springtime of the year when the sun shines and the days begin to warm. After a seed starts to grow, the embryo grows into a young plant. Seedlings need warm temperatures, water and food to keep growing.

VII. Management Suggestions
To inhibit mold growth on the seeds, rinse seeds with a weak bleach solution (5 ml of bleach in one liter of water). Have students wash hands before planting seeds.

VIII. Procedure
1. Distribute a lima bean seed or a red bean to each student.
2. Tape a dampened paper towel inside a Ziplock bag and place a seed on the paper towel as shown on the worksheet.
3. Place the sealed Ziplock baggies in a dark area (inside desks or in the closet). Predict how long it takes for the bean to sprout.
4. Predict which part will appear first: the root or the stem.
5. After the bean sprouts, hang the bags in the window with tape or on a bulletin board with push pins. The students will observe that the beans have roots that grow toward the floor and stems that grow toward the sky.
6. Predict and record how many days it will take for the first leaves to appear.
7. Predict how long the cotyledons (food supply for the young plant) remain on the plant before falling off.

8. Draw the plants as they grow.
9. Measure the stem and root growth each day and graph the results.

IX. Discussion
1. Describe the growth of the roots and the stem. How do they compare in length, color, direction?
2. Keep a daily observation log and describe the daily changes.
3. How did you provide for the needs of the seed for growth?

X. Extensions
1. Compare other seeds to the lima bean seeds.
2. Construct a plant growth view box. Remove the top from a small milk carton. Cut a window in the side of the carton. Cover the window with plastic wrap. Fill the carton with soil and plant seed next to the window. Keep the flap closed, and open only to view the seed growing.

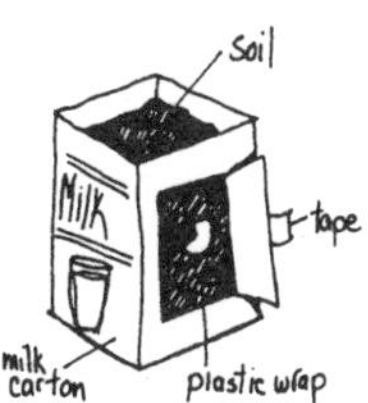

3. Use three beans; place them as shown on the drawing. Will the different placement of the seeds effect the germination of the seeds?
4 Mix a cup of plaster of paris with water. Pour into a styrofoam cup. Place a dry lima bean in the middle of the mixture. When the plaster of paris is dry, peel the cup from around it. Set it on a shelf and watch what happens. (The lima bean should swell from the moisture in the plaster of paris and crack the plaster.)

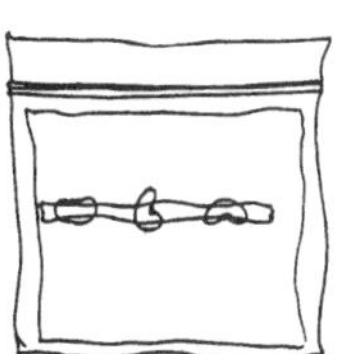

A Seed Grows

______________ Scientist

	Prediction	Actual
1. Will the root or stem sprout first?	______	______
2. How many days will it take for the beans to sprout?	______ days	______ days
3. How many days will it take for the first leaves to grow?	______ days	______ days
4. How much do the roots grow each day?	______ cm	______ cm
5. How much does the stem grow each day?	______ cm	______ cm

6. What else did you observe about your growing bean plant?

____

____

____

____

____

____

A Seed Grows

Scientist ______________

Place a lima bean in a bag. Use the next page to make your predictions about its growth. Measure the growth each day. Draw the plant as it grows.

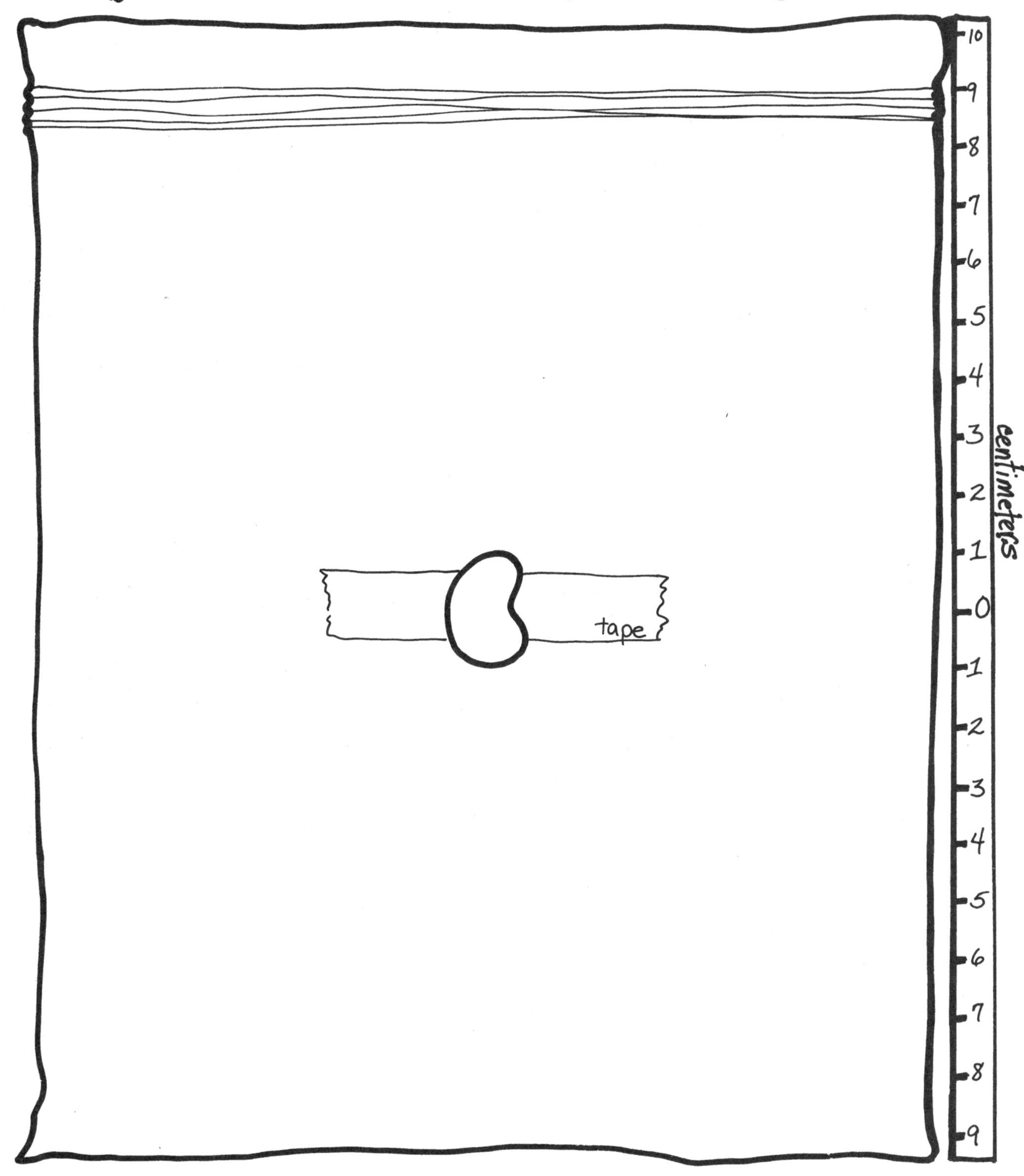

A Seed Grows

____
Scientist

How much does your seed grow each day? Measure the length of the stem and the root daily. Color the graphs to match the lengths.

Stem

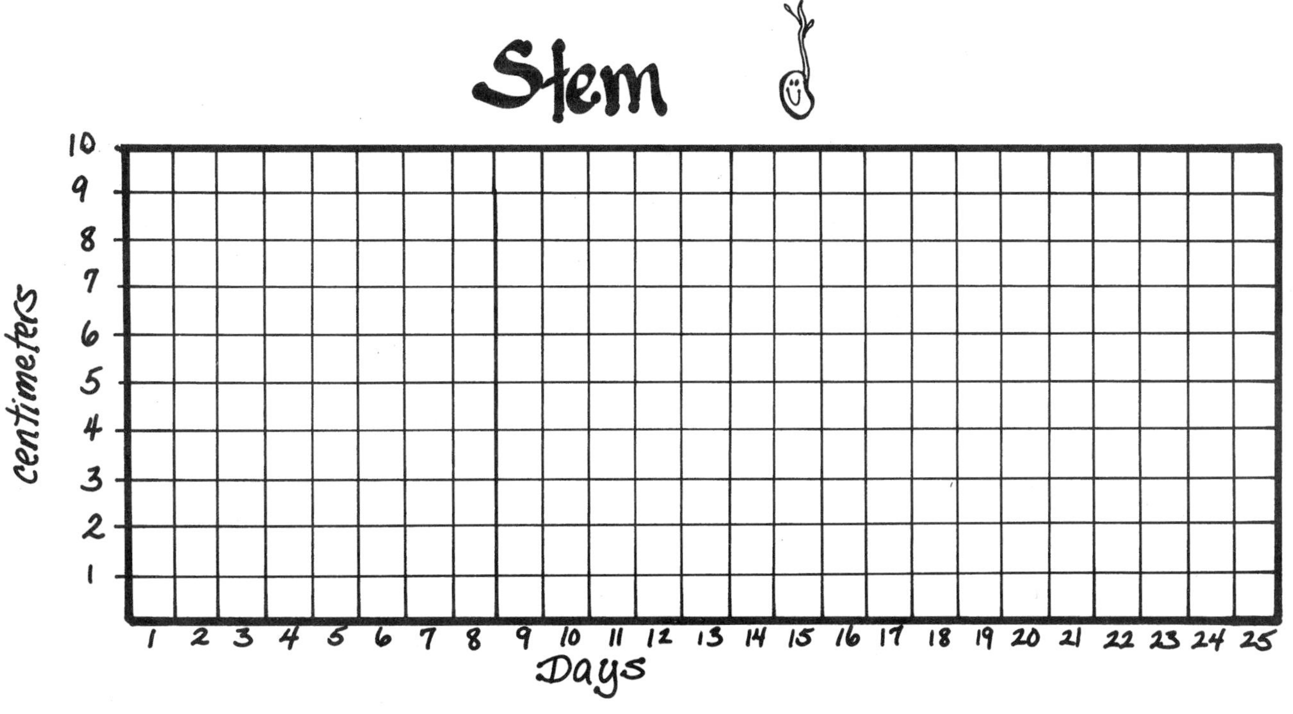

Root

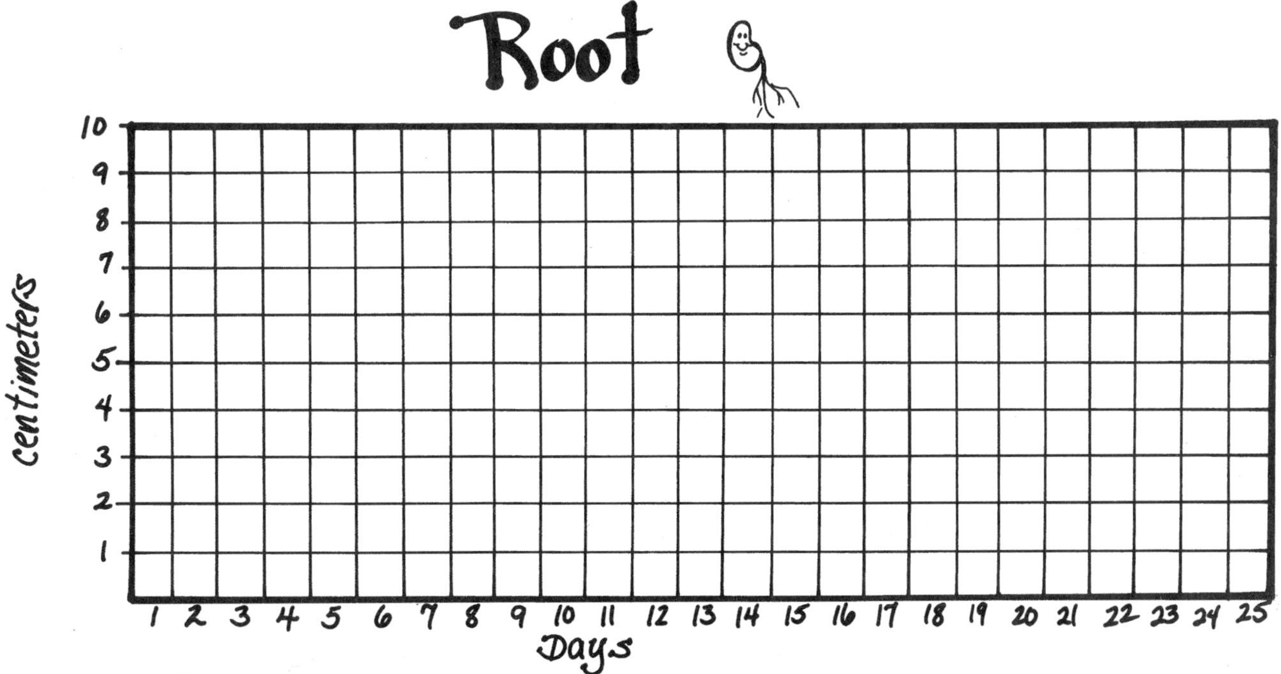

A Plant Begins

You will need:

Seeds (lima, corn, or radish)
Potting soil
Booklet
Container (plastic pot, styrofoam cup, or milk carton)

Do this:

1. Prepare the pot and potting soil.

2. Plant the seeds.

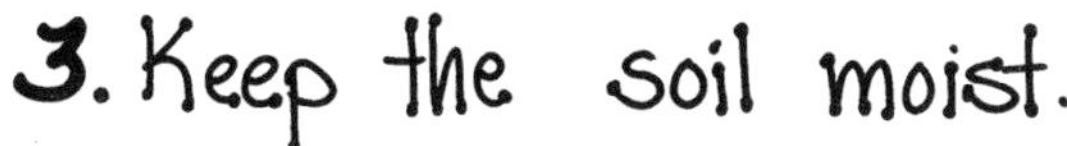

3. Keep the soil moist.

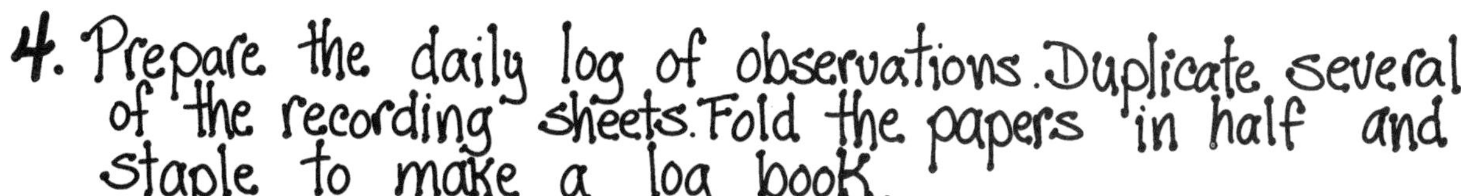

4. Prepare the daily log of observations. Duplicate several of the recording sheets. Fold the papers in half and staple to make a log book.

5. When the seeds sprout and grow above the soil, start recording the growth by drawing and writing your observations.

6. Continue recording observations every few days.

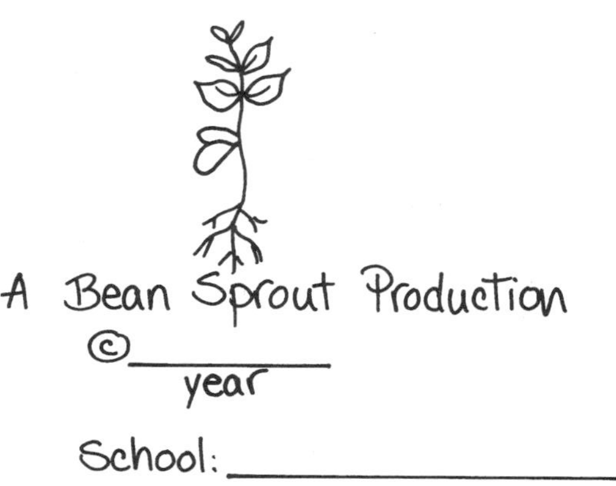
A Bean Sprout Production
©________
year
School: ____________

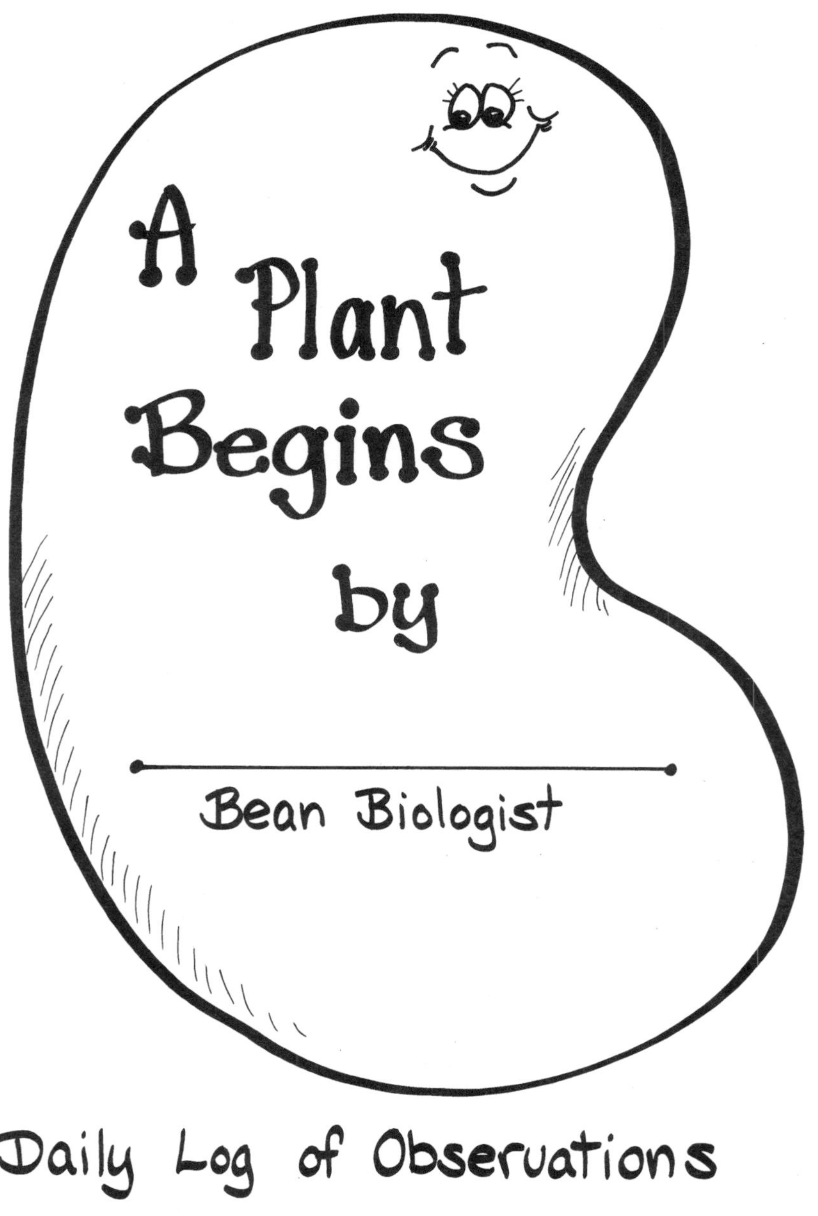
A Plant Begins by
Bean Biologist
Daily Log of Observations

Drawing

Make a Terrarium

You Will Need: Plastic 2 liter bottle
Scissors
Potting Soil
Plant or plant cutting

Do This:

1. Cut the top from the 2 liter bottle with scissors. (Save and use later as a funnel.)
2. Pull the hard plastic bottom free from the bottle. You may need to soak in warm water first.
3. Put pebbles in the bottom of the hard plastic bottom. Add potting soil.
4. Gently place your plant into a small hole in the soil. Cover the roots with soil and add water.
5. Turn the clear plastic upside down into the hard plastic bottom.
6. Watch your plant grow. Make sure it gets plenty of light. Add water if needed.

It's in the Bag

I. Topic Area
Biological Science: Plants—a baggie garden

II. Introductory Statement
Students will "plant" seeds in a plastic Ziplock type bag and observe and measure the growth of roots, stems and leaves.

III. Math Skills
a. Measuring
b. Comparing

Science Processes
a. Recording Data
b. Observing
c. Measuring

IV. Materials
Assorted seeds: lima beans, kidney beans, corn, sunflower seeds, garbanzo beans, etc.
Clear plastic baggies—Ziplock type—one for each student
Transparent tape or double sided tape
Paper towels (school restroom type)

V. Key Question
What does a seed look like as it starts to grow?

VI. Background Information
The production of seeds is the last stage of reproduction of flowering plants. When fertilization takes place, the ovules of a flower become seeds. These are called embryos which means new developing plant. Surrounding the embryo is a layer of cells called the endosperm where food is stored for the embryo to use later.

The outer layer of the ovule becomes the seed coat, the skin that provides protection for the seed. When seeds leave the parent plant, they become dormant until just the right conditions of warmth and water cause the seeds to germinate.

VII. Management Suggestions
1. While many hands-on activities work well with students working in pairs or small groups, this activity is most successful where each student has a "baggie" of his very own for the "growing" part. Teachers will need to provide enough baggies and seeds for this.
2. When selecting an assortment of seeds, use medium to large size seeds. The broad bean type are easier for young students to handle.
3. Placing seeds in a moist warm environment (in the baggie) may encourage additional growth—mold, etc. Rinsing seeds in a very weak bleach solution (1 tsp. bleach to a gallon of water) will inhibit unwanted mold growth.
4. Make several copies of the page "How My Seeds Grow" so the students can staple the pages together to make a booklet.

VIII. Procedure
1. Choose two seeds that are different from each other, such as a lima bean and corn or garbanzo bean and popcorn.
2. Fold a paper towel to fit inside a small plastic baggie. Use double sided tape and place the seeds on the tape, or run transparent tape across the two seeds to hold them in place on the wet paper towel.
3. Wet the paper towel and slip it into the baggie and seal. It will not be necessary to water the seeds again.
4. Tape the bags to the window or hang them on a line along the windows. Watch the roots grow down and the stem and leaves grow up.
5. Make measuring rulers to attach to the front of the baggie by printing the page "How My Seed Grows". Tape the centimeter rulers to the outside of the baggie, making sure that the 0 mark is lined up with both the seeds.
6. Make a small picture book "How My Seeds Grow". Observe growth, and record daily or every other day, depending on how rapid growth changes occur.
7. Transplant seeds to a pot or terrarium after they seem to grow out of the bag.

IX. Discussion
1. Which seed do you think will sprout first? Why?
2. Which came first, the root or the stem?
3. Why is it unnecessary to add water to the closed baggie?
4. Describe how the seeds get water, light and food in the bag.

X. Extended Activities
See "Make A Terrarium". Plant a seed or transplant your seedling to a plastic one- or two-liter bottle.

How My Seeds Grow

Plant a mini-garden in a Zip Lock bag. Print extra copies of this page. Cut on the solid lines and staple to make a record book. After the seeds begin to sprout, have children record the growth by drawing every other day. Children can predict which seed will sprout first and which one will grow the fastest. Lima beans and popcorn work well.

Day:

Day:

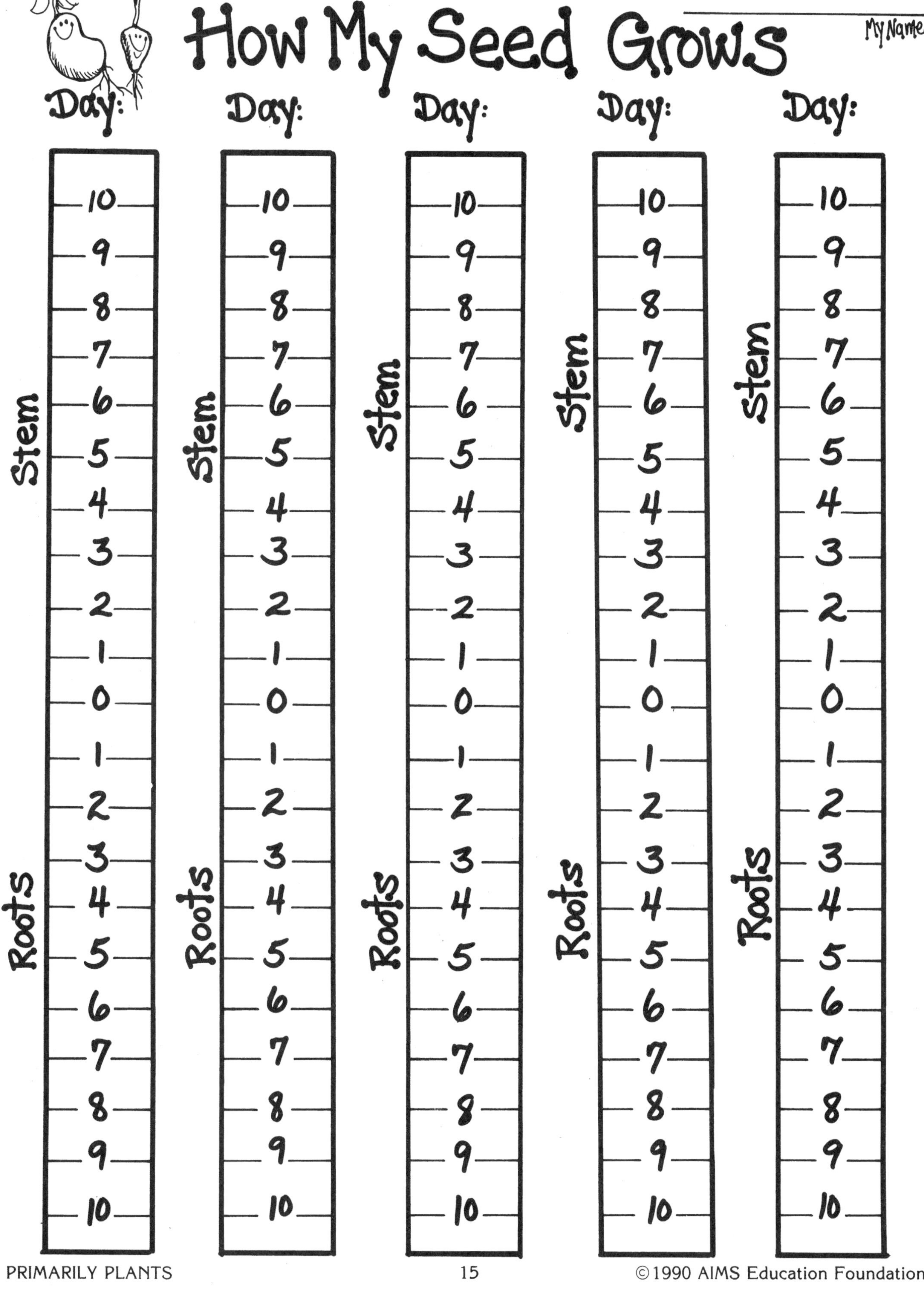
How My Seed Grows
My Name
Day:
Day:
Day:
Day:
Day:
Stem
Roots
10
9
8
7
6
5
4
3
2
1
0
1
2
3
4
5
6
7
8
9
10

Little Brown Seeds

As students are learning about seeds and growing plants, they can learn the poem "Little Brown Seeds".

Little Brown Seeds

Little brown seeds so small and round
Are sleeping quietly underground.
Down came the raindrops
Sprinkle, sprinkle, sprinkle.
Out comes the rainbow
Twinkle, twinkle, twinkle.
Little Brown seeds way down below
Up through the earth they grow, grow, grow.
Little green leaves come one by one.
They hold up their heads
And look at the sun.

1. Print the pages of the booklet. Cut the pages in half and have students put them in sequential order.
2. Students can color the pictures or glue construction paper cut outs and the actual seeds and soil on the pictures.
3. Students can choral read the poem with some of them performing a pantomime of the growth of a seed. Participants can curl up as seeds, then slowly sprout, stretch and unfurl their leaves as they grow taller and taller.

"Author Unknown"

Little
Brown
Seeds

Little brown seeds so small and round,
Are sleeping quietly under ground. 1.

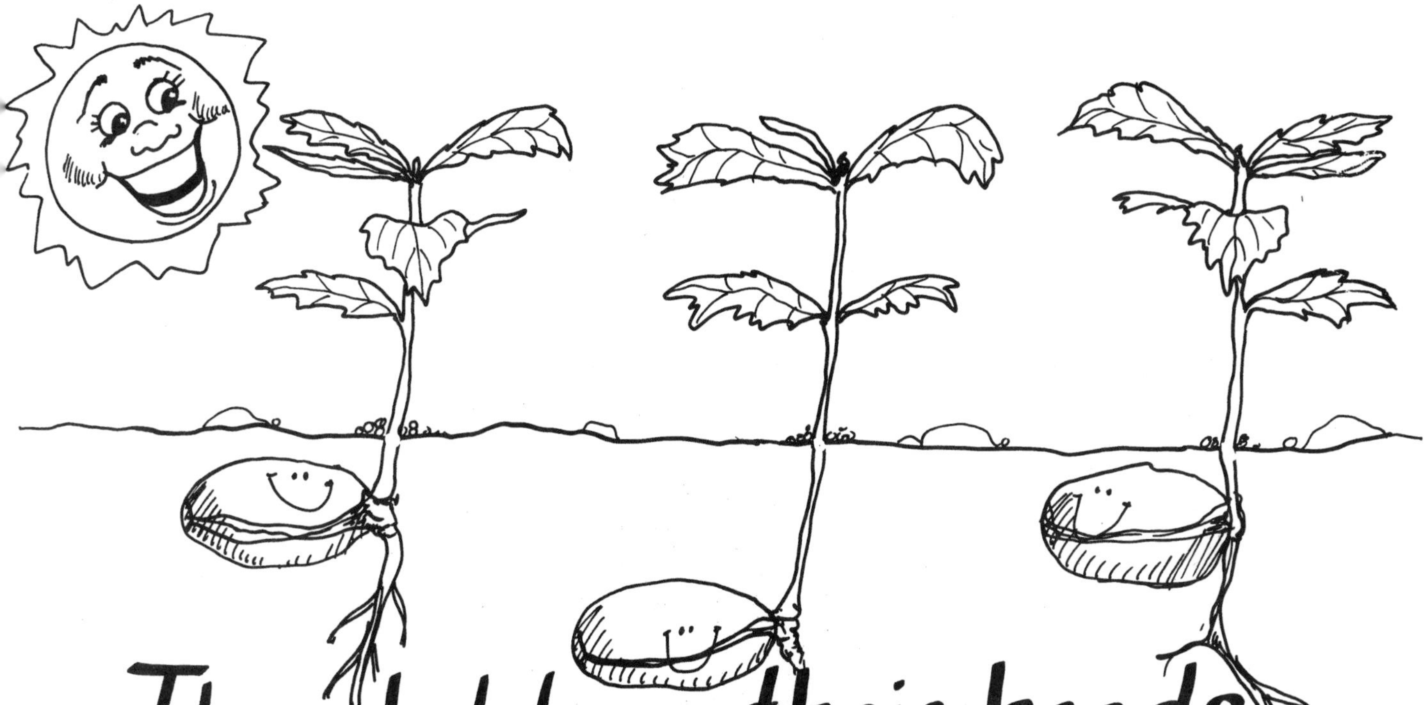

They hold up their heads
and look at the sun. 6.

Down come the raindrops
sprinkle, sprinkle, sprinkle.

2.

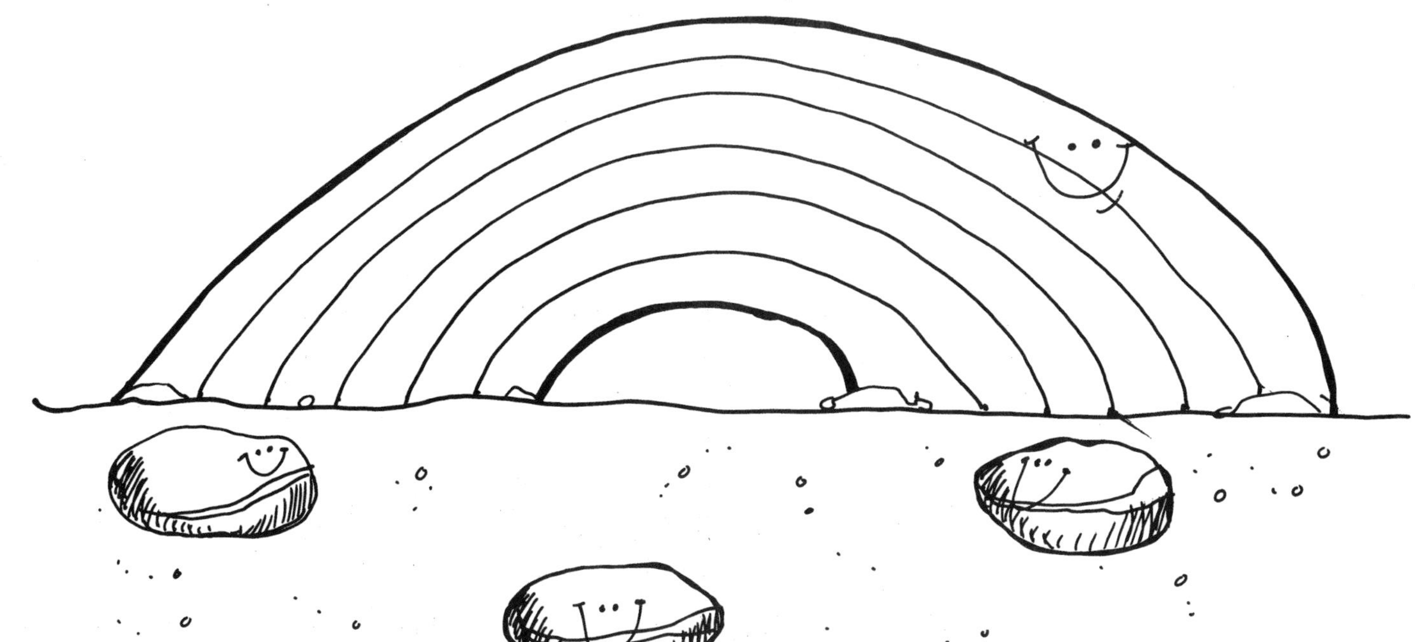

Out comes the rainbow,
twinkle, twinkle, twinkle.

3.

Little brown seeds way down below
Up through the earth they grow, grow, grow.

4.

Seeds, Spores, and More.

A seed is a tiny case containing plant life. It contains a small plant and food. Seeds come in all different sizes and shapes, but when you open a seed case, you will find that every seed contains a tiny plant called an embryo. The seeds contain food to sustain the tiny plant until it can make its own. The food storage is called the cotyledon. Some plants such as a bean have two cotyledons. Others, such as corn, have only one cotyledon.

Nearly all trees, shrubs, vegetables, and flowers started as seeds. Some of the seeds grow into seedlings and then into adult plants. Very few seeds actually survive, so plants produce an enormous number of seeds to insure reproduction of the plant.

When a seed is ripe, it drops from the parent plant. It starts to grow or germinate when it has water, warmth, and air. A root appears first and grows downward. Then a stem pushes upward towards the light. The first leaves appear and the plant can make its own food in its leaves.

There are many kinds of seeds that we eat. Perhaps the most important plants in the world are grasses. Wheat, oats, corn, and rice are different kinds of grasses called cereals. The seeds of these cereals provide food for many of the animals we eat.

There are also nonflowering plants such as ferns, mosses, and algae that produce spores. A spore is a cell with a thick, protective covering, much smaller than the smallest seed. Spores do not include an embryo, so they develop directly into an adult plant. When conditions are right, spores are distributed by air or water.

On the underside of fern leaves you can find small brown lumps. These lumps produce spores. When the spores are ripe, they fall to the ground and grow into new ferns.

Seed Sort

I. Topic Area
Biological Science: Seeds

II. Introductory Statement
Students will count and sort seeds and find the likenesses and differences of many seeds.

III. Math Skills
a. Measuring
b. Counting
c. Estimating

Science Processes
a. Sorting & Classifying
b. Observing
c. Recording
d. Comparing

IV. Materials
Small Dixie cups—one per group of 3-4 students
Assorted seeds: lima beans, kidney beans, popcorn, sunflower seeds, garbanzo beans, black-eyed peas, etc.
Magnifying lens

V. Key Question
How are seeds alike and different?

VI. Background Information
Seeds are all different sizes and shapes and they come surrounded by all different kinds of fruit. But all seeds are alike in two ways. Every seed contains a little plant called an embryo. All seeds contain food that helps the little plant grow.

All seeds are remarkable in the way in which they spread themselves in order to grow new plants. Some seeds simply fall to the ground, others float on water, some are fired like buckshot over a distance and others attach to an animal's fur.

All seeds serve the same purpose, to germinate and grow a new plant in order to perpetuate the plant species.

VII. Management Suggestions
1. It is important for this activity to get at least 5 or 6 different kinds of seeds. Be sure they are different sizes so they can be easily sorted. 7 bean soup mix works well.
2. The students should be placed in groups of 3-4.

VIII. Procedure
1. Provide an assortment of seeds. Mix the seeds together so the students can be given a representative sample.
2. Place the students in groups of 3-4 and give each group a small cupful of seeds.
3. Have the students estimate how many seeds are in the cup.
4. Give each group a copy of the worksheet "Seed Sort".
5. The students will dump the cup of seeds into the circle in the middle of the paper and sort the seeds into smaller sets of like kinds and put them in the smaller circles.
6. A record should be made of the name and number of seeds in each circle.
7. Then have the students add the smaller sets to get the total number of seeds in the cup.
8. Have the students use a magnifying lens to look closely at the seeds. What color are they? Are there any that have two colors? The students can record their answers on the sheet "Observing Seeds".
9. Ask the students: "What are the shapes of the seeds?" Have them record by drawing the shapes of the seeds in the shapes column.
10. Have the students guess how many seeds it will take to cover the line. Lay the seeds on the line, count them and record.
11. The students will use the worksheet "Comparing Seeds" to weigh the seeds. They should estimate how many seeds it will take to balance one teddy bear and then weigh the seeds and record the results. At the bottom of the page record by coloring the graph.

IX. Discussion Questions
1. Of which seed type were there the most in your group? the least?
2. How are the seeds alike? How are they different?
3. What color are the seeds?
4. Are the seeds all the same shape?
5. Are they all the same size?

X. Extension
1. Plant the seeds.
   a. See if the students can identify which plant came from which seed.
   b. Which seed sprouted first?
   c. Which plant has the longest leaves?
   d. How do the plants differ?
2. Use the seeds to create a picture.

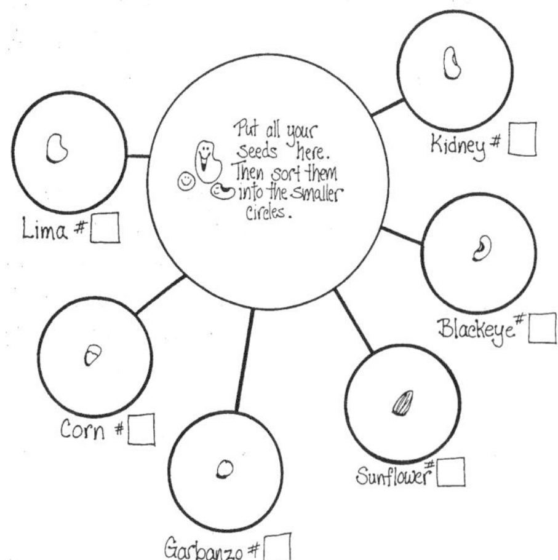

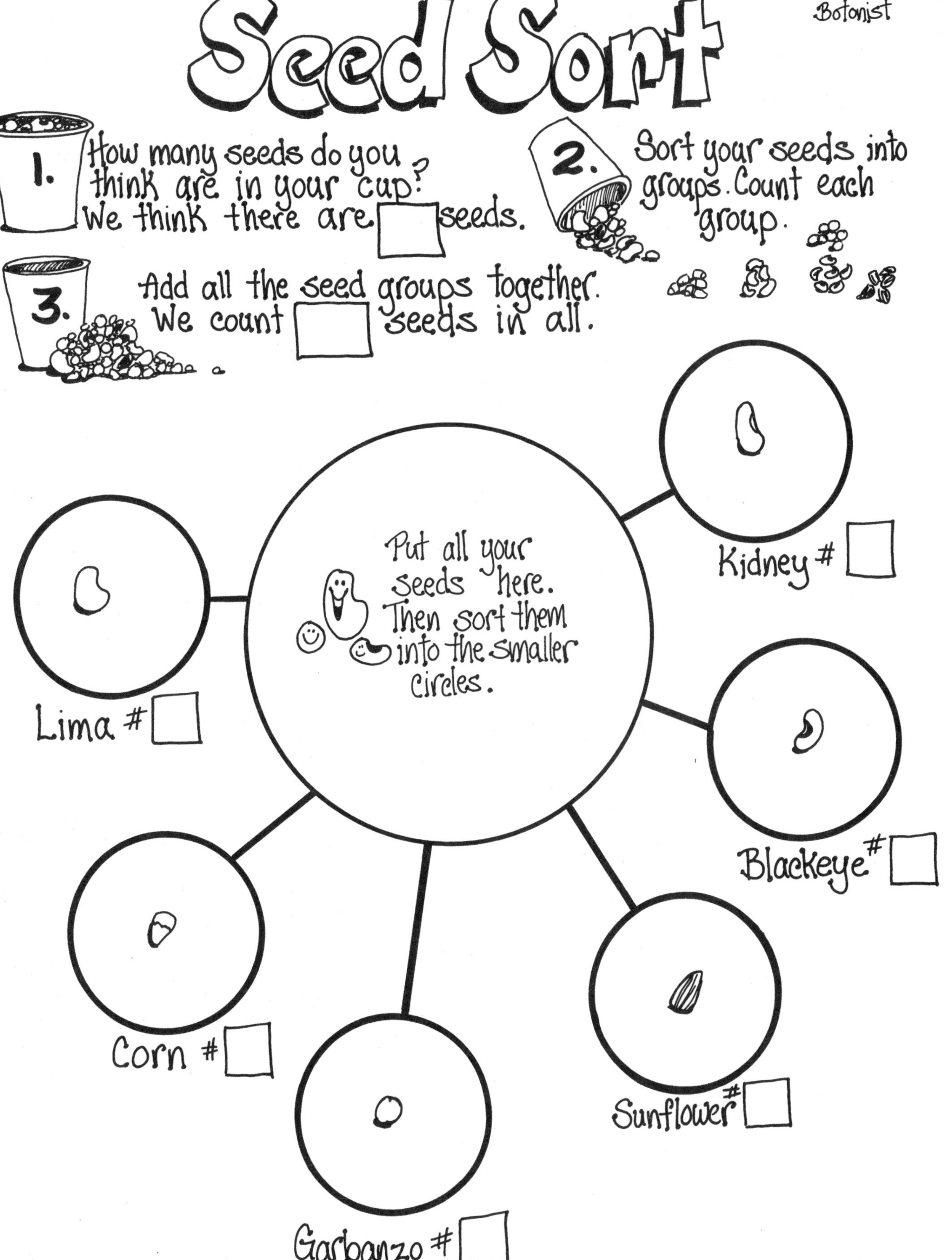
Botanist
Seed Sort
1.
How many seeds do you think are in your cup?
We think there are seeds.
2.
Sort your seeds into groups. Count each group.
3.
Add all the seed groups together.
We count seeds in all.
Put all your seeds here. Then sort them into the smaller circles.
Kidney #
Lima #
Blackeye #
Corn #
Sunflower #
Garbanzo #

Botonist ____________

Comparing Seeds

How many of each seed will balance one teddy bear?

	I think:		I count:
Lima	______		______
Garbanzo	______		______
Corn	______		______
Sunflower	______		______
Blackeye	______		______
Kidney	______		______

Color the graph to show what you found out.

	1	2	3	4	5	6	7	8	9	10	11	12	13	14	15	16	17	18	19	20
Lima																				
Garbanzo																				
Corn																				
Sunflower																				
Blackeye																				
Kidney																				

Number of seeds to balance 1 teddy bear.

Botanist

Observing Seeds

Look closely at your seeds. Name the colors that you see. Draw the shapes of the seeds.

	Colors	Shapes
Lima		
Garbanzo		
Corn		
Sunflower		
Blackeye		
Kidney		

How many seeds does it take to cover this line?

	I think:	I count:
Lima	______	______
Garbanzo	______	______
Corn	______	______
Sunflower	______	______
Blackeye	______	______
Kidney	______	______

The Seed Within

I. Topic Area
Biological Science: Seeds

II. Introductory Statement
Students will compare size, shape, and color of various seeds.

III. Math Skills
a. Counting
b. Shapes
c. Sequencing

Science Processes
a. Observing
b. Collecting/Recording Data
c. Comparing

IV. Materials
Fresh fruits and vegetables—oranges, apples, lemons, bell peppers, melons, tomatoes, peas, avocado, peaches
Sharp knife
Paper towels and paper plates
Students pages

Apple
# of seeds
Shape of seeds

V. Key Question
How do the seeds vary in size, color and number in each fruit or vegetable?

VI. Background Information

Seeds are made in the fertilized ovule of a flower. Once a flower has been pollenated, seeds begin to develop. The part of the flower that holds the seeds starts to grow bigger. This part becomes the fruit, the protective structure surrounding the seeds. Plant species survive because of the seeds the fruit protects.

The fruit can be fleshy and moist like apples, melons and tomatoes or hard and dry like nuts and beans. The sweet, juicy and brightly colored fruits are readily eaten by animals and so the seeds are scattered far from the parent plant. Although we use the terms fruits and vegetables for the protective structure surrounding the seeds, in reality all of them are fruit of the plant.

VII. Management Suggestions
1. Collect the fruits and vegetables that you wish to use.
2. Divide the students into groups; part of the group could remove the seeds, the other part could count the seeds.
3. Each group needs a half of a tomato, bell pepper, apple, orange, a slice of the melon and a whole peach, avocado, and pea pod (these can be shared by the groups).
4. Buy valencia oranges or use lemons.
5. If the worksheet on the outline of fruit is too small, cut it in half and enlarge the fruit outlines.
6. K-1 teachers could use just one fruit a day. The fruit outline could be enlarged to page size or a large outline on the wall. The seeds could be glued on the fruit outline.
7. Have the students record the number of seeds in each fruit by coloring in on the graph, then make a large graph to use on the wall and the students could glue their seeds on it.

Peas
# of seeds
Shape of seeds

VIII. Procedure
1. Introductory discussion
   a. How do plants start?
   b. Where do we get the seeds?
   c. Do all fruits and vegetables have the same number of seeds?
   d. Why do some fruits and vegetables have many seeds and others have just a few?
   e. Are all seeds the same size?
   f. In what ways are seeds the same or different?
2. Show the students the various fruits and vegetables. List them on the board or transparency.
3. Ask the students what they think the insides look like.
4. Cut the fruits and vegetables and distribute the pieces to the students for observation. Allow time for the students to observe their fruits.
5. Students should record where the seeds are located on their student page.
6. Students will count the seeds and record the number and shape on the worksheet.
7. The class results can be recorded on a wall chart or transparency.
8. Wash and dry the seeds. Graph the number of seeds by gluing to a large class graph.

Bell Pepper
# of seeds
Shape of seeds

IX. Discussion
1. Where were the seeds located?
2. How were the seeds different?
3. What shape are the seeds?
4. How many seeds does each fruit or vegetable have?
5. Do all large fruits and vegetables have large seeds? What about small fruits and vegetables?
6. Which fruits have many seeds in them?
7. Which fruits have only one seed in them?
8. Can you think of a large fruit or vegetable that produces a small seed? (watermelon)
9. Is there a small fruit that has a large seed? (avocado)

X. Extensions
1. Students could try growing the seeds they remove from the fruits and vegetables. The avocado seed makes a nice plant.
2. Have the students make fruit salad with the fruit they have been exploring.
3. Sequence seeds from largest to smallest.

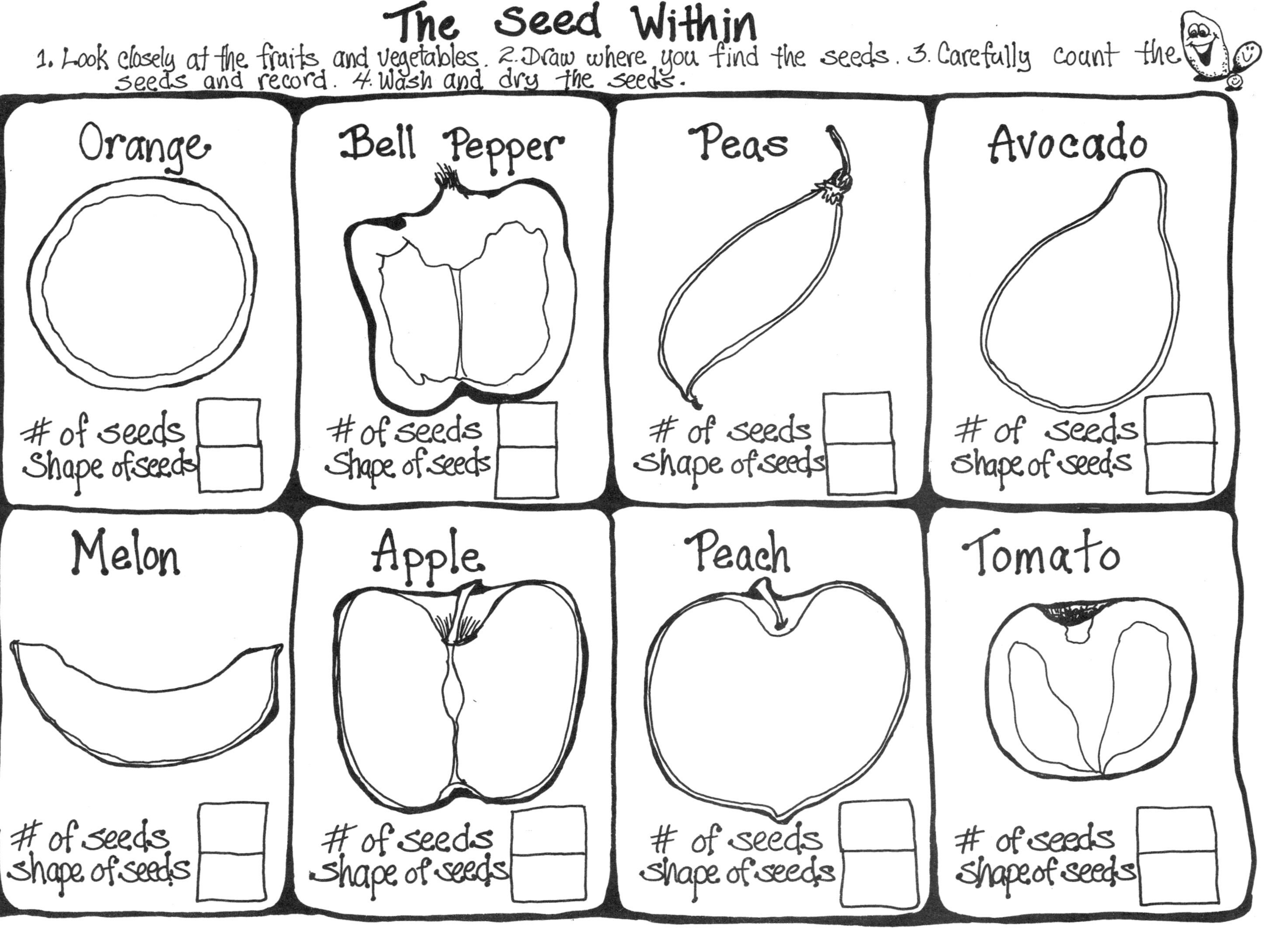
The Seed Within
1. Look closely at the fruits and vegetables. 2. Draw where you find the seeds. 3. Carefully count the seeds and record. 4. Wash and dry the seeds.
Orange
# of seeds
Shape of seeds
Bell Pepper
# of seeds
Shape of seeds
Peas
# of seeds
Shape of seeds
Avocado
# of seeds
Shape of seeds
Melon
# of seeds
Shape of seeds
Apple
# of seeds
Shape of seeds
Peach
# of seeds
Shape of seeds
Tomato
# of seeds
Shape of seeds

The Seed Within

1. Look closely at the fruits and vegetables. 2. Draw where you find the seeds. 3. Carefully count the seeds and record. 4. Wash and dry the seeds.

# of seeds
shape of seeds

# of seeds
shape of seeds

# of seeds
shape of seeds

# of seeds
shape of seeds

# of seeds
shape of seeds

# of seeds
shape of seeds

# of seeds
shape of seeds

# of seeds
shape of seeds

Botanist ______________________

The Seed Within

Color your graph to show the number of seeds in each.

Orange	Bell Pepper	Peas	Avocado	Melon	Apple	Peach	Tomato

Seeds Travel

I. Topic Area
Biological Science: Seed Dispersal

II. Introductory Statement
Students will observe many ways that seeds travel from the parent plant.

III. Math Skills
a. Measuring
b. Identifying Attributes

Science Processes
a. Observing
b. Recording Data
c. Sorting and Classifying

IV. Materials
Assorted seeds that travel by wind (dandelion, milkweed, maple, sycamore, pine), by water (cranberry, coconut), by animal fur (cocklebur, crabgrass, beggar-ticks, thistle)
Magnifying glass

V. Key Question
How many ways can seed be dispersed by a parent plant?

VI. Background Information
Most plants produce a large number of seeds. This is because so few seeds survive. In order to ensure survival many seeds are modified in various ways so they can be carried away from their parent plant.

Some fruit and seeds simply drop from a parent plant. They take root there, but have competition for space and light.

Many seeds have developed wings or silky hairs that allow them to be carried by the winds for miles. The dandelion seed, for example, has a little parachute which helps it to be carried by the wind.

Plants that grow along the banks of streams and rivers often have seeds that will float on water. The seeds usually have tough husks and air spaces in the seed to help them float. The best known seed that floats many miles is the coconut.

Many seeds have sharp hooks or barbs which stick to animals with furry coats like sheep or dogs. They drop off some distance from where they grew.

Seed dispersal helps to prevent too many seedlings from growing in a small area near the parent plant. Those plant species that are able to spread their seeds widely have a better chance of surviving.

VII. Management Suggestions
1. This lesson will use only three of the many ways that seeds are dispersed. These three are ones that students enjoy and can observe best.
2. Collect seeds from the different ways of seed travel—wind, water or animal fur. Or use other categories that suit your environment.

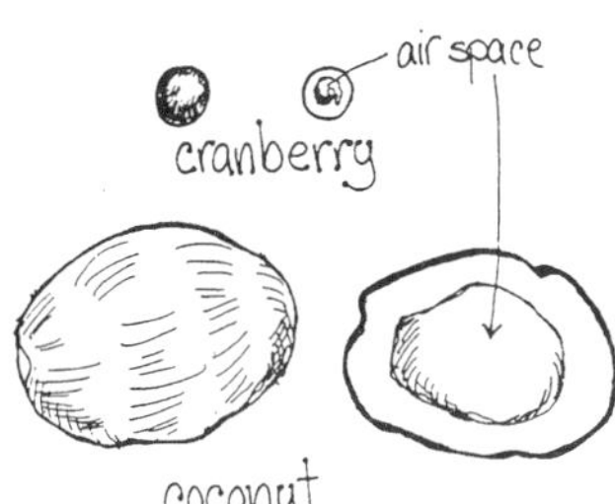

3. This lesson needs to be taught in the fall season when many seeds can be collected, or the seeds can be collected to use later in the year.
4. To find seeds look around your school. The trees planted along the streets near the school will produce seeds. Weeds often survive along the edges of the playground, or find a wild environment or vacant lot.

VIII. Procedure
1. Read the information sheet "Seed Travels" with the students.
2. Collect seeds that are carried by animals' fur. With a magnifying glass have the students look at the tiny hooks or barbs on the seed pod. See if the students can imagine how these tiny fruits hook a ride with animals with fur. Each hooked bract has a seed at the bottom.

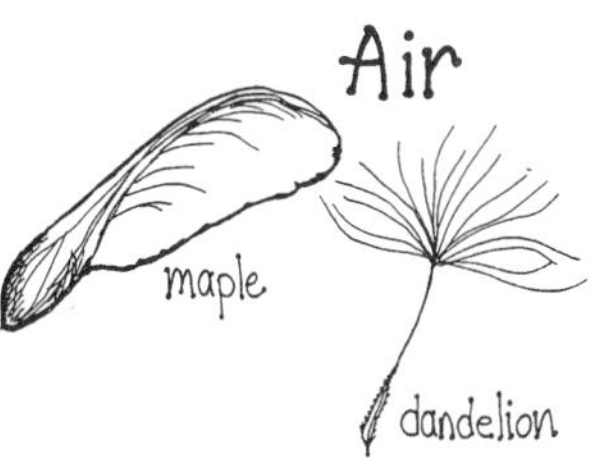

3. Collect seeds that produce a "parachute"; bull thistle, milkweed, dandelion are some. The students should use a magnifying glass to examine the seed at the bottom of the parachute. Encourage the students to let the seeds blow in the wind to see how far they will go before landing. You might encourage a race.

4. The maple, linden, ash, and pine tree seeds have wings. These will resemble helicopters as they travel towards the ground. If your school has a second story, drop the seeds from an upper window and watch the miniature "helicopter". See how far it travels. Otherwise, just toss the seed in the air and watch it land. Open the helicopter to see where the seeds are held.
5. The best known floating seed is the coconut; however, a smaller floating seed is the cranberry. Look at the waxy waterproof coat of the cranberry. Cut it open and examine the four air pockets, each of which contains a seed. Some seeds if they land on moving water will be carried quite a distance; however, this is not the primary means of dispersal for most seeds.
6. Have the students record what they see when they study these seeds on the worksheet "Seeds Travel".

IX. Discussion Questions

1. How far can winged seeds fly? Do they need a strong wind?
2. Why do the seed cases (fruit) differ with the various dispersal methods?
3. Which do you think is the most efficient mode of travel for the seeds?
4. What is the best kind of weather for airborne seeds to disperse?
5. Can you find some other way in which seeds are dispersed than the ways that have been studied?

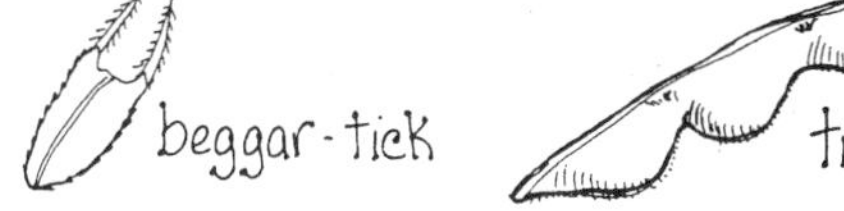

X. Extension

1. Have the students collect as many kinds of seed as possible and classify them into various ways of travel.
2. Write a story about a seed that travels far from the parent plant.
3. Make collages with the seeds that have been collected.
4. Make paper helicopters. Do they fly the same way that nature's seed helicopters do?
5. Choose some flowering plant in the spring. Watch it carefully. What happens when the petals fade? Where does the fruit form? What happens to the seeds? Go back in the fall. How are the seeds scattered, by the wind, by animals, or by water?
6. Invent a seed that has an unusual way of traveling from the parent plant.
7. Use "Helicopters and Parachutes" worksheet as an extension to the section on seeds carried by air.

Seeds Travel

Seeds cannot move by themselves. They must be carried away from the parent plant so they have enough light and space to grow.

Hitchhikers

Some seeds have hooks or hairs that catch on people's clothes or animals' fur. These seeds "hitchhike" a ride far from the parent plant.

cocklebur

beggar-tick

tick trefoil

foxtail

Water

Some plants that live near water have seeds that float. The seeds drop into the water and float away from the parent plant. Some have spaces inside to help them float. Any seed that floats can be carried by water.

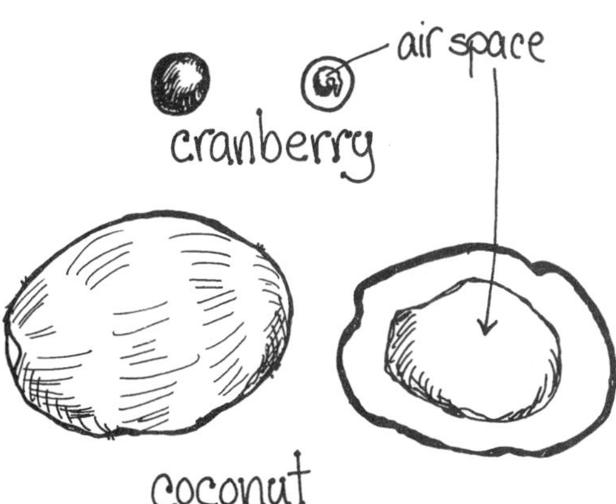

Air

Many light seeds have wings or silky hairs that help them to be carried by the wind. The hairs catch the wind like a parachute. The ones with wings turn like a helicopter as the seeds ride the wind away from the parent plant.

maple

dandelion

milkweed

Seeds Travel

Botonist

Collect seeds. Look at them carefully with a hand lens. Decide how each one travels. Place seeds into groups. Draw each seed and glue the seed next to your drawing.

Hitchhiker (sticks)

How do these seeds hitchhike?

Water (floats)

What makes these seeds float?

Air

Helicopter (wings)

Parachute (hairs)

How are these seeds carried by the wind?

My Name: ______________________

Helicopters and Parachutes

Find 2 seeds that can travel by wind. Draw them.

1.

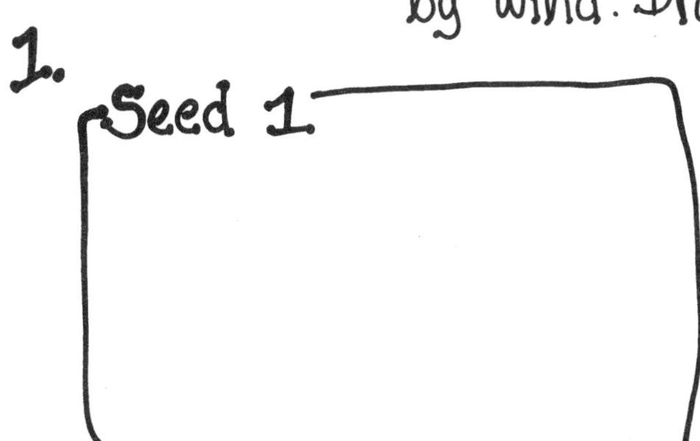

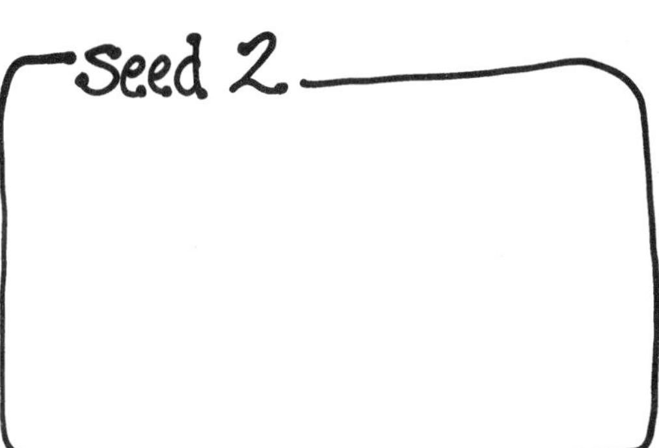

2. Hold the two seeds over your head and drop them at the same time. Which one stayed in the air longest? (circle one)

Seed 1 Seed 2

3. How long can each seed stay in the air?

Seed 1: __________ seconds Seed 2: __________ seconds

4. Go outside when a breeze is blowing. Drop both seeds. Which seed travels the farthest? (circle one)

Seed 1 Seed 2

5. How far did each one travel?

Seed 1: __________ cm Seed 2: __________ cm

Observing Bulbs

I. **Topic Area**
Biological Science: Plants—Bulbs

II. **Introductory Statement**
Students will observe another way for plants to reproduce.

III. **Math Skills**
a. Measuring

Science Processes
a. Observing
b. Recording

IV. **Materials**
Bulbs—onions, garlic, daffodils, tulips, narcissuses
Potting soil
Pots

V. **Key Question**
How does a bulb grow?

VI. **Background Information**

Bulbs are a special type of plant. They consist of a round, underground structure that develops in some plants. The bulb is made up of thickened layers of fleshy leaves, which hold the stored food. In the center is a large bud scale that produces the new plant. Roots grow from the solid basal plate. The outer scales form a dry and papery covering.

The purpose of the bulb is to store food. When the plant is growing, it stores food in these fleshy underground leaves. When the winter comes the above ground plant dies, but the bulb with its stored food remains alive underground. When the new growing season begins, the bulb's central bud sends out a shoot, which produces a stem, leaves and flowers above the ground. Food stored in the bulb starts the new plant's growth.

Onions and garlic are perhaps the food bulbs most familiar to the students. Tulips, daffodils and narcissuses are garden flower bulbs.

VII. **Management Suggestions**
1. The garden flower bulbs can be bought in the fall in nursery stores. Onions and garlic are available anytime in a grocery store.
2. Put the students in groups of 3-4.
3. Winter is a nice time to force flower bulbs into blooms.

VIII. **Procedure**
1. Provide enough bulbs (onion, daffodil, narcissus, tulip) so the students can see and handle a bulb.
2. Tell the students to observe the bulb carefully, using their sense of seeing, hearing, feeling, and smelling.
3. Have the students give words that describe their bulb. The teacher can record the words on the board or on a large piece of butcher paper.
4. Discuss with the students that a bulb consists of fleshy food storage leaves. A stem with leaves and flowers will come from the center of the bulb.
5. Plant the bulbs; keep them well watered and in the sunlight. The students can enjoy watching the bulbs grow and flower.
6. Some daffodil bulbs can be grown indoors in bowls of pebbles and water. Keep in the dark and cool until growth is well along, then bring slowly into the light.
7. Leave an onion in the dark for several weeks. The onion will sprout and send out long green leaves and roots. The thick scale leaves of the bulb will become soft and the onion is no longer good to eat. The students can see how the food supply of the bulb has been used to grow the new leaves and roots.

IX. **Discussion**
1. What is the purpose of the thick fleshy underground leaves of a bulb?
2. Where do the roots of the bulb come from?
3. What color are bulbs?
4. What do bulbs feel like?

X. **Extension**
Plant a white narcissus bulb in a clear plastic cup, with gravel and water. Keep in the dark until growth is started, then put the pot in a sunny window. These plants with their pretty white blooms cheer up a gray winter day and are nice gifts to send home.

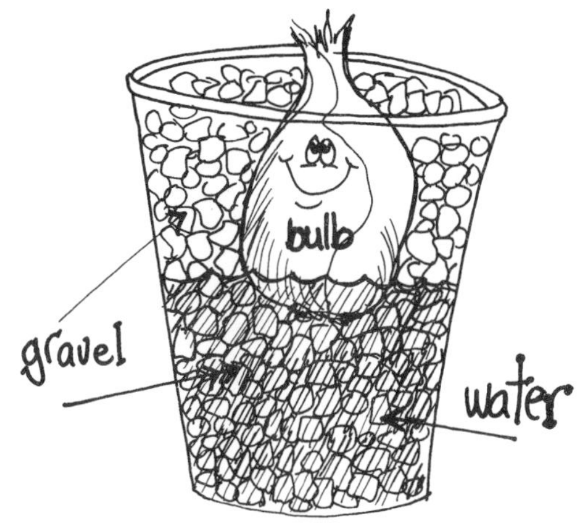

Scientist ______________________

Observing Bulbs

Use your senses to observe your bulb. Draw and describe what it looks like.

1. Observations

My bulb is a ______________________

Looks: ______________________

____

Smells: ______________________

____

Feels: ______________________

____

2. Drawing

3. Use your notes to write a description of the bulb.

____

____

____

____

____

____

____

Plant a Bulb

You will need:

white narcissus bulb
small gravel
water
cup (16oz.)

Do this:

1. Fill a cup half full of gravel. Put the bulb inside, then add more gravel until the cup is full.

2. Add enough water to touch the bottom of the bulb.

3. Place the bulb in a sunny window. Watch it grow.

4. How many days will it take to sprout?

I think______days. I count______days.

5. After the bulb begins to grow, measure its height each day.

Day Number

1	2	3	4	5	6	7	8	9	10	11	12	13	14

Height

Cuttings

I. Topic Area
Biological Science: Plants—Other ways to start plants.

II. Introductory Statement
Students will observe that plants can be grown by other means than by the germination of seeds.

III. Math Skills
a. Measurement

Science Processes
a. Observing
b. Measuring

IV. Materials
Philodendron or coleus cuttings
Clear plastic glasses
Plastic bag
Carrot top or beet top

V. Key Question
Can plants be grown from cuttings? How do cuttings grow?

VI. Background Information
Plants can reproduce in another way other than by the germination of seeds. They can turn "cuttings" of themselves into new plants. When a plant reproduces this way, the young plantlets are genetically identical to the parent.

VII. Management Suggestions
1. The philodendron plant or coleus plant are perhaps the easiest to grow from cuttings.
2. For the best cutting material, look for healthy, normal tip growth. With a sharp knife cut a 4 to 5 inch-long stem, making the cut just below a leaf; remove all leaves on the lower half of the stem.
3. Fill the clear plastic glass with water and place the stem of the cutting in the glass. Keep the cuttings out of direct sunlight.
4. Have the students bring a carrot top or a beet top for this activity. The tops should be cut off with a half inch of the fruit or vegetable left on it.

VIII. Procedure
1. Take a cutting from a coleus or philodendron plant.
2. Cut off the stem with a sharp knife just above one of the leaves. Make another cut under the lowest leaf.
3. A plant will put out new roots right at the leaf node (where the leaf sprouts from the stem). Cut off the lower leaves.
4. Have the students use a magnifying glass to see the leaf bud on the stem.
5. Put the cutting in a glass of water. Put a plastic bag (with air holes) over the glass.
6. Watch! In about a week, roots will start to grow from the bottom of the cutting and leaves will sprout from the leaf node.
7. When the roots are about an inch in length, the cutting can be planted in soil.
8. Put the cutting in a pot and fill with soil, pressing down firmly. Leave enough room so the plant can be watered.
9. Leave the plastic bag over both the plant and the pot for about a week, until the roots have gotten used to their new home.
10. Watch your new plant grow!
11. Another way to grow new plants is to use the tops of carrots or beets. The tops must be cut with a half-inch of the body of the fruit or vegetable left on.
12. Plant each top in a pot. Cover them with soil so that just the very top part sticks out.
13. Soon small leaves start poking up. Under the soil roots will be growing.
14. In about two weeks, a little beet "tree" and a carrot "bush" will be growing.

IX. Discussion
1. Why is growing a new plant from cuttings better than growing a plant from seeds? (The new plant will be genetically identical to the parent plant.)
2. From what part of the stem do the roots start to grow?
3. What other fruits or vegetables besides carrots and beets can you find that can grow new tops?

X. Extensions
1. Try growing a begonia or African violet plant from a leaf.
2. Grow a sweet potato vine. Push 3 toothpicks firmly into the sweet potato at equal distances around the tuber; these will support the potato within the rim of the glass. Keep the water level so it just touches the tip end of the tuber. Sprouts will grow from the potato and in 6 weeks you will have a vine with attractive foliage.

Plants from Cuttings

You will need: containers (cups, clear glass, or clay pots)
potting soil
plant cuttings (philodendron or coleus)
vegetable cuttings (carrot or beet top)
water

Do this:

1. Cut a philodendron or coleus stem just below one of the leaf nodes. Trim the lower leaves.
2. Put the cutting in a glass of water.
3. Watch for roots and leaves to grow from the cutting.
4. Put the cutting in a pot and fill with soil. Press down firmly and water when needed.

Another Way

1. Cut ½ inch from the top of a carrot or beet.
2. Plant the top of the vegetable in a pot. Cover with soil so just the very top sticks out.
3. Keep the soil moist and watch for growth.

Spores: A Special Seed

I. Topic Area
Biological Science: Plants—Ferns and Mosses

II. Introductory Statement
Students will observe spores, a special seed, from which ferns and mosses are reproduced.

III. Math Skills
a. Comparing
b. Identifying Attributes

Science Processes
a. Observation
b. Recording Data

IV. Materials
Fern fronds with spores
Magnifying lens

V. Key Question
Where do spores grow? What do they look like?

VI. Background Information
Ferns and mosses are two of an important group of green plants that do not form true seeds. They form spores that take the place of the seed, in a flowering plant, and develop into a young plant.

The leaves of ferns are called fronds. If you look at the undersides of some fronds, you will see some dark brown spore cases. When the spores are ripe, they blow away on the wind. One fern plant may produce millions of spores.

When a fern spore lands on a moist, shady ground and has ideal conditions, it begins to grow. The young plant is shaped like a tiny heart. The little plant is called a prothallus. Soon a small fern begins to grow from the upper surface.

VII. Management Suggestions
1. This activity is best done during the late summer or fall months when spores form on fern plants. Collect some fern fronds with brown spores on the underside of the leaves.
2. The diagram used is of a sword fern frond because these spore cases are the easiest seen. However, there are many other kinds of fern that can be used.

VIII. Procedure
1. Look at the top of a fern frond and describe it.
2. Carefully turn the frond over. Are there small bumps on the leaf?
3. Using a magnifying lens, look at the bumps and describe them.
4. Draw the spore cases (brown bumps) on the diagram of the fern leaf.
5. Count the number of spore cases on a leaf. How many are there?
6. How many spore cases can you find on one frond?

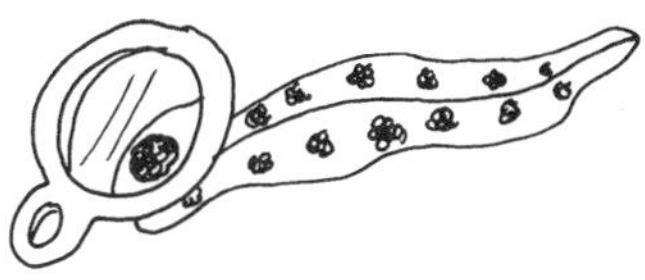

7. Are there the same number of cases on each of the leaves?
8. Compare the number of spore cases on the leaves at the top of the frond with a leaf further down on the frond.
9. Are there spore cases on each leaf of the fern frond?

IX. Discussion
1. What do the spores look like? What color are they?
2. Why do the spores appear on the underside of the leaves?
3. Why does a plant produce so many spores?
4. How else do ferns spread?
5. What is a fungus that produces spores that we consider a delicious food? (mushrooms)

X. Extensions
1. Have the students investigate the number of different ferns around their school and homes. There are nearly 10,000 different kinds of ferns in the world. They could make a collection of the kinds of ferns they found.
2. Make fern prints or fern rubbings. Make fern printings on T-shirts.

Fern Frond

____
My Name

A fern is a green plant that grows from spores not seeds.

1. Observe a fern frond. Count its leaves.

My frond has________leaves.

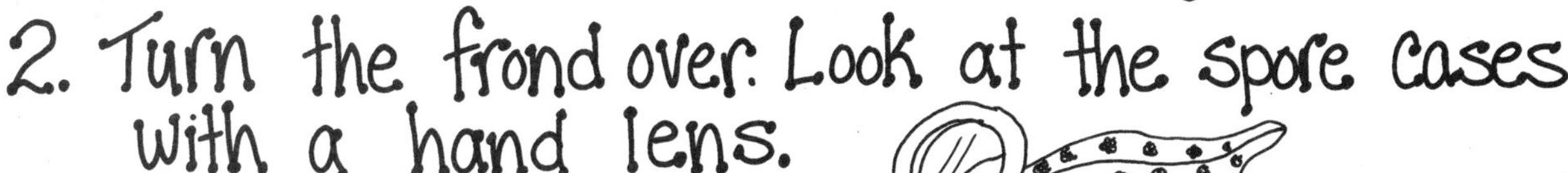

2. Turn the frond over. Look at the spore cases with a hand lens.

3. Pick a leaf about this size. Draw the spores on this leaf.

There are________spore cases on the leaf.

4. Pick a small leaf at the top of the frond and a large one at the bottom of the frond.

Compare.

Small leaf	Large leaf
length ________	length ________
# spore cases ________	# spore cases ________

Plant Needs

Plants are organisms that grow and reproduce their own kind. They need food, air, soil, water, light, and space to grow.

Plants need soil. Water and minerals are taken from the soil through roots. Soil also provides support for the plant and an anchor for the roots to grow in. Decaying plants and animals leave behind minerals in the soil that are essential for future plant growth.

Plants need sunlight in order to grow properly. They use light energy to change the materials - carbon dioxide and water into food substances (sugars). This process of food production is called photosynthesis. Only in light can a green plant make food.

Plants must also have clean air. Green plants take in carbon dioxide from air and use it during photosynthesis to make food. Dirty, smoggy air blocks sunlight that plants must have.

Plants need water. Water is essential to all life on earth. No known organism can exist without water. Plants use water to carry moisture and nutrients from the roots to the leaves and food from the leaves back down to the roots.

food water

Plants must also have space in order to grow. Plants are found everywhere - deserts, mountains, arctic regions, forests, jungles, oceans, and even in cracks of sidewalks of busy cities. If the space is small, the plants will be small and stunted. Big plants need big spaces for their roots and branches.

Which soil works best?

I. Topic Area
Biological Science: Plants—Soils

II. Introductory Statement
Students will plant seeds in a variety of soils to see which soils provide the best medium for plant growth.

III. Math Skills
a. Measuring

Science Processes
a. Observing
b. Comparing
c. Recording Data

IV. Materials
Clear plastic 9 oz. tumblers
Potting soil
Sand
School yard "dirt"
Clay
Water
Large bean seeds

V. Key Question
Which soils are good for growing plants?

VI. Background Information

Soils provide the water and minerals that a plant needs. Without soil, the plant can be watered, but it becomes difficult to give the plant the nutrients that it gains from the soil. Soil also provides support for the plant and its root system.

Soil usually has three separate layers. The top layer contains minerals and humus, the decayed remains of animals and plants. Humus and minerals are needed by plants for good growth. The second layer contains humus and minerals that have been leached from the top soil. The third layer consists of rocks that are being broken down to form soil.

A great helpmate to the enrichment of soil is the earthworm. Earthworms burrow through the soil and leave castings of digested leaves and other matter which help enrich the soil. They also improve the soil with their tunneling by making it easier for air and water to soak in. Earthworms do not make poor soil into good soil, but rather they keep the soil in good condition for growing.

VII. Management Suggestions

1. Students may wish to work in pairs or teams of three or four to plant and observe four sets of seeds.
2. Teamwork also makes it appropriate for "jobs" to be assigned. They may all wish to keep a daily log of activity and then compare notes.

VIII. Procedure

1. Use four clean clear cups per team. Fill each one three-fourths full with different types of soil: potting soil, sand, playground "dirt" and clay. Plant a bean seed in each cup, placing the seed up against the clear side wall of the cup for easy viewing. Add measured amount of water to each cup and record.
2. Predict and record what you think will happen in each cup.
3. Allow time for seeds to grow. Illustrate the results.
4. Compare results and discuss. Draw conclusions regarding best medium for growth.

IX. Discussion

1. How are all the types of soil alike? How are they different?
2. Why do you think one might be better than another for growing bean plants?
3. Discuss the difference between germination and actual plant growth.
4. How shall we decide which seed grew the best? Which kinds of things do we look for? size of plant? color? number of leaves?
5. Does more than one kind of soil produce a good plant?
6. Could soils be combined to make a better growing bed?
7. Can plants grow without soil? How?

X. Extensions

1. Create a new soil mix and test it.
2. Write a poem or a story about seeds and soil.
3. Use adjectives to describe soil: rough, sandy, earthy, etc.
4 Write a soil poem.

Soil
Earthy
Sandy
Rough
Loamy
Smells good.

Playground Soil

Which soil works best?

Plant a seed in each cup. Water and watch them grow. Draw what happens to each seed.

What do you think will happen? ______________________

What happened? ______________________

Plants and Water

I. Topic Area
Biological Science: Plant Needs—Water

II. Introductory Statement
Students will investigate whether or not a plant needs water to live.

III. Math Skills
a. Measuring

Science Processes
a. Observing
b. Comparing
c. Recording

IV. Materials
Water
Clear plastic glasses
Plants
Potting soil

V. Key Question
Can plants grow without water?

VI. Background Information

Water is perhaps the most important substance to life on earth. No known organisms can exist without water.

Plants, like every other living thing, need water in order to live and grow. Water carries the dissolved minerals and nutrients from the soil to the plant, and carries food from the leaves back down to the roots.

The plants get water in several ways—through rainfall, irrigation, and dew. In our homes we water our plants. Most plants get water from rain. Even in the desert areas plants would die without moisture.

VII. Management Suggestion

Buy two plants of the same size, variety and same type pot. Use plants grown in the previous lesson.

VIII. Procedure

1. Have the students describe what they observe about each plant. Draw the plants if possible.
2. Put both plants in a sunny spot on the window sill in view.
3. Water one plant every day for five days. Do not water the other plant.
4. Have the students predict what they think will happen to the plants. (When a plant gets no water, it cannot make food. Without food the plant will die.)
5. Draw a picture of what happened.

IX. Extensions

1. Put radish or marigold seeds (fast growing) on two sponges. Wet one and keep it damp. Keep the other dry and observe the differences that occur.
2. To show that roots take up water from the soil, test with a potato. Peel the bottom half of the potato and cut the end flat so it can stand. Dig a hole in the top part. Stand the potato on its flat end in a dish of water. Watch! The potato will soak up water and fill the hole in the top.

_______________ 

Plants and Water

Use two plants. Water one but not the other.

What do you think will happen? _______________

Draw what the plants looked like after a week.

water 	no water

What happened? _______________

Plants and Sunlight

I. Topic Area
Biological Science: Plant Needs—Sunlight

II. Introductory Statement
Students will be able to prove that a plant needs light in order for it to develop correctly.

III. Math Skills
a. Comparing

Science Processes
a. Observing
b. Communicating

IV. Materials
Sunflower seeds (any alternative seed will do)
Potting soil
Flower pots or plastic containers
Box
Aluminum foil
House plant
Two plants the same size

V. Key Question
Do plants need sunlight in order to grow?

VI. Background Information

Plants need food and can make their own food. But they need things from which to make their food. Green plants need carbon dioxide from the air, water and minerals from the soil, and energy from the sun.

Only in light can a green plant make food. The process of food-making is called photosynthesis. In photosynthesis, the carbon dioxide and water are changed to carbohydrates and oxygen. Food can only be made in the presence of chlorophyll. Chlorophyll is the substance responsible for a plant's green color.

When a green plant is deprived of sunlight, it soon loses its chlorophyll. It cannot make food, so it dies.

VII. Management Suggestions
1. Use sunflower seeds or any fast growing seeds.
2. Remember, the first leaves are not the true leaves; wait for the second set of leaves.
3. For number 5, be sure that the plant is healthy and receives good care during the time one leaf is covered by aluminum foil.
4. Get two plants of the same size.

VIII. Procedure
1. Soak the sunflower seeds overnight. Then plant three sunflower seeds in each pot and put them near the window. Water the pots well. Now cover one pot with the cardboard box.
2. When the first true leaves appear on the plants that are uncovered, remove the box from the other pot.
3. Discuss with the students what happened to the plants. Why did the sunflower seed under the box not grow? Do plants need light to grow? Do they need light to remain healthy?
4. When a plant gets no sunlight, it cannot make food. Without food the plant will die. Use two plants of the same size. Cover one with a box or place it in a closet to block out all light. After one week without light, bring the plant out and compare it to the one that received sunlight. The plant that did not receive sunlight will lose some of its green color. It will not look as healthy as the other plant. Make sure it now receives sun and watch for it to return to health.
5. Observe the leaves of a healthy house plant. Cover one of its leaves with aluminum foil so that it does not receive sunlight. Leave covered for a week, then uncover and observe the changes. The leaf should be pale compared to other leaves on the plant.

IX. Discussion
1. What happens to a plant that has no sunlight?
2. Do plants need light in order to grow?
3. What do the leaves produce when they receive sunlight?
4. What color are the leaves of the plant that doesn't receive sunlight?

X. Extension
1. Put a potato in a dark, warm spot for several weeks. What happens to the potato? If left in the dark for several months, will the potato die? Try it.
2. Lay three or four seeds in the bottom of a shallow bowl and place a wet sponge over them. Keep them damp. When the seeds sprout, watch to see what happens to them. Turn the dish. Do the seedlings turn toward the light?
3. Put a rock or a board on a patch of grass, leave it for two weeks. Take the rock off and observe. What has happened to the grass? Is it a different color from the surrounding grass? Has the grass died? Now leave the rock or board off the grass. Does the green color return to the grass?
4 Write a plant log about one of the experiments.
5. Let the students make up an activity of their own with plants and sunshine.

Plants and Space

I. Topic Area
Biological Science—Plant Needs—Space

II. Introductory Statement
Students will understand that plants grow in many places and need space.

III. Math Skills
a. Comparing

Science Processes
a. Observing

IV. Materials
Two large pots
Radish seeds or any fast growing seeds
Water

V. Key Question
Do plants need space in order to develop correctly?

VI. Background Information

Plants are found everywhere—gardens, lawns, forests, flower pots, hillsides, or in the water. Plants can even be found in cracks in the sidewalk and cracks in tar. If the spaces are small, plants will be small. If the spaces are large, the plants tend to be large. Plants can grow up, down, around a tree, across the soil, in the water and in almost all kinds of places.

VII. Management Suggestions
1. Use small seeds that grow fast.
2. Prepare two pots with soil.

VIII. Procedure
1. Have the students look out the window and answer the question, "Where do plants grow?" (List answers on the board.)
2. Ask—"Do all plants need the same amount of space to grow in?" (no) Why not?
3. Compare the amount of space a tree needs for growth against that of a grass plant.
4. Prepare two pots with soil. Plant both with radish seeds. Give both pots the same amount of water and sunlight. Leave the pots alone for 12 days.
5. In one pot leave all the plants that are growing.
6. In the second pot thin the baby plants until only three or four are left.
7. Give the pots water and sunlight as before for another 10 days. Then compare the growth and the roots of the plants in both pots.

IX. Discussion
1. Ask the students to explain what was done differently to the plants in the two pots. Why are the plants in the pot that has been thinned so much larger and healthy looking? (They have fewer plants to share the water and chemicals in soil.)
2. What happens to trees when there are too many trees crowded together? (They are spindly.)
3. Ask the students how they feel when they are crowded on a bus or in a room and can't move. Do they like it? Do they think it is always healthy?

Plants and Space

Name ____________________

1. Plant the same amount of radish seeds in each cup (about 20). Cover with soil.
2. Give the same amount of water and light to both cups.
3. After 12 days, thin plants from one cup so there are only 4 left. Leave the other cup alone.
4. What do you think will happen? ____________________

____

5. After 3 weeks, draw what happened to the plants.

6. Why do you think this happened? ____________________

____

What do Plants Need to Grow?

I. Topic Area
Biological Science: Plants—What do plants need to grow?

II. Introductory Statement
Students will understand that in order to grow healthy plants, soil, water, light and air must be provided.

III. Math Skills
a. Measurement

Science Processes
a. Observation
b. Comparing
c. Recording data

IV. Materials
Milk cartons—from school lunches
Bean, radish or corn seeds
Potting soil mixture

V. Key Question
What do plants need to grow?

VI. Background Information
Plants require sunlight, water, soil, and air in order to grow and be healthy. Energy received from the sun is used to convert carbon dioxide and water into food. When plants do not receive the things they need to live and grow, they will either die or be stunted in their growth.

VII. Management Suggestions
1. Save the ½ pint milk cartons from the students' lunches, rinse them out and cut the tops off.
2. Use fast growing seeds such as radish, corn, or bean seeds.

VIII. Procedure
1. Gather enough ½ pint milk cartons from the cafeteria for the class.
2. Cut the top off the milk carton.
3. Fill the carton with a soil mixture.
4. Choose seeds that sprout fast, such as radish, bean, or corn.
5. Plant the seeds in the milk cartons. Dampen the soil.
6. After the seedlings sprout, divide them into four different groups.
7. Subject them to different growing conditions.
8. Condition #1—Plant has soil, water, and air but does not have light. Put these plants under a box or in the closet.
9. Condition #2—Plant has soil, light, and water but no air. Seal these plants in a large clear plastic bag.
10. Condition #3—Plant has soil, light, and air but no water. Do not water these plants.
11. Condition #4—This is the control group. The plants have soil, air, light and water.
12. When the seedlings come through the soil, measure each week how much the plants have grown in each environmental condition.
13. Record each on a separate graph.
14. After several weeks compare the graphs. Are there differences in rate of growth of the different plants in the separate condition?

IX. Discussion
1. Discuss with the students what each plant needs in order to grow. (soil, air, light, and water)
2. Have the students explain what the plants look like in each of the conditions and what need was lacking in each one.

X. Extensions
1. Have the students decorate the sides of the milk cartons with paper, roving, yarn, etc. and use them as pots for their plants.

What do Plants Need to Grow?

You will need: 4 milk cartons
soil
radish, bean, or corn seeds
scissors

Do This:

1. Cut off the top of the milk cartons to make planters.
2. Decorate with roving or paper.
3. Fill the cartons with soil.
4. Plant the seeds in the soil. Dampen the soil.
5. Wait. After the seeds sprout, divide the cartons into 4 groups to test growing conditions.
6.

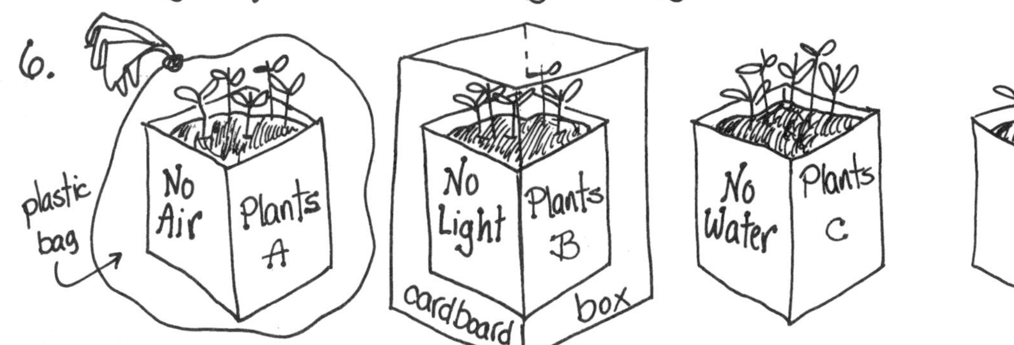

Has: soil, water, light No Air	Has: soil, water, air No Light	Has: soil, air, light No Water	Has soil, air, light and water

7. Watch to see which plants grow best. What do plants need to grow?

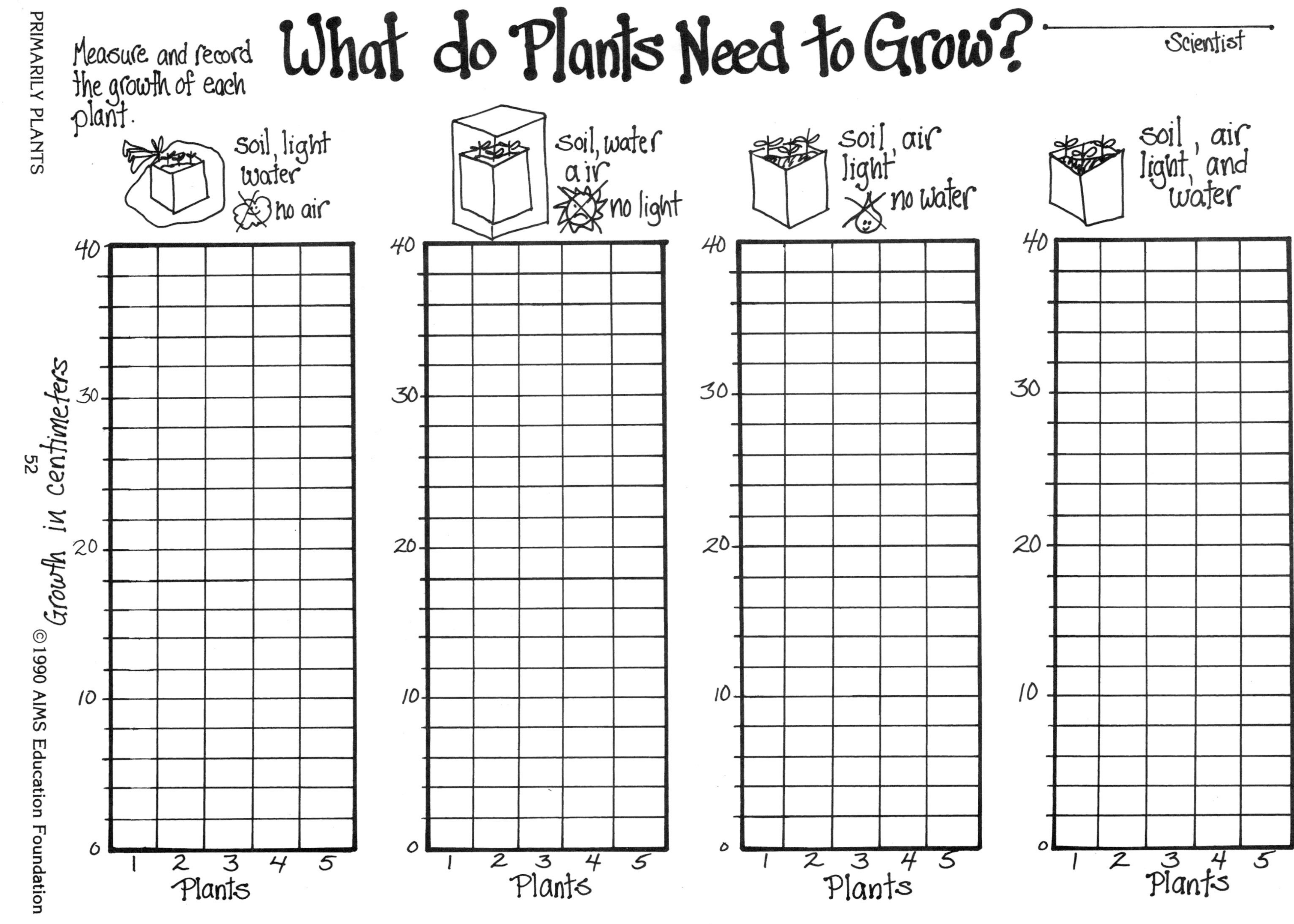
What do Plants Need to Grow?
Scientist
Measure and record the growth of each plant.
soil, light water no air
soil, water air no light
soil, air light no water
soil, air light, and water
Growth in centimeters
0
10
20
30
40
Plants
1 2 3 4 5

What Temperature is Best?

I. Topic Area
Biological Science—Plant Needs—Temperature

II. Introductory Statement
Students will realize that plants are affected by extremes of temperature.

III. Math Skills
a. Prediction

Science Processes
a. Observation

IV. Materials
Three similar plants
Heater (if activity is done in winter)
Ice chest
Ice

V. Key Question
How do plants react to temperature extremes?

VI. Background Information
Different kinds of plants live in different places. The temperature, length of season, and amount of rainfall help to determine the kinds of plants that will grow in a place.

Proper conditions for plant growth can be created on farms and in greenhouses.

Plants can be found in deserts where it is hot and dry. They grow in the forest and in grassland areas. Type of soil, amount of water, sunlight, and temperature help determine what kinds of plants live in any one place.

VII. Management Suggestions
1. If possible, this activity should be done during the hot weather. If it is done in the winter, place plant near a heater.
2. Use a refrigerator or freezer, if possible, for the cold environment.
3. Get three healthy house plants that are similar in size.

VIII. Procedure
1. This activity should be done during hot weather, if possible.
2. Get three similar healthy house plants. Start with the soil around the plants moist.
3. Be certain the students realize that all three plants are essentially the same.
4. Place one plant outside where it is hot, preferably in the direct sunlight. (If this experiment is done in the winter, place the plant near a heater.)
5. Place another one of the plants in a cold environment, such as a freezer. (If a refrigerator is not available, use an ice chest filled with ice.)
6. Place the third plant in a moderate environment such as the classroom.
7. Discuss with the students what they think will happen to the plants.
8. Have them predict which plants will be healthy at the end of the experiment.
9. Observe the plants for five days.
10. Draw how the plants looked at the beginning of the experiment and at the end of the experiment.

IX. Discussion
1. Discuss with the students that in nature plant growth adjusts to different temperatures and rainfall. Many plants that live here can not survive in the cold arctic regions or in the hot desert areas.

____
Scientist

What Temperature is Best?

1. Get 3 plants that are alike. Give each plant the same amount of water.

2. Draw each one.

1	2	3

3. Put plant # 1 where it is hot-in the sun.
   Put plant # 2 where it is cold-in the freezer.
   Put plant # 3 where it is moderate-in the classroom.

4. What do you think will happen? _______________

____

5. Observe the plants for 5 days. Draw the plants.

1	2	3

6. What did you learn about how temperature affects plants? _______________

____

What do Plants Need?

Use the booklet "What do plants need?" as a culminating activity for the section on plant needs.

Have students color or decorate the booklet as they wish. Place on the class library shelf for free reading or send home for students to read to their families.

It is also possible to enlarge the booklet to 11"x17" and use as a class Big Book. Read each page as the class participates in an activity that matches. The class practices reading pages each day until they can read the entire book on their own.

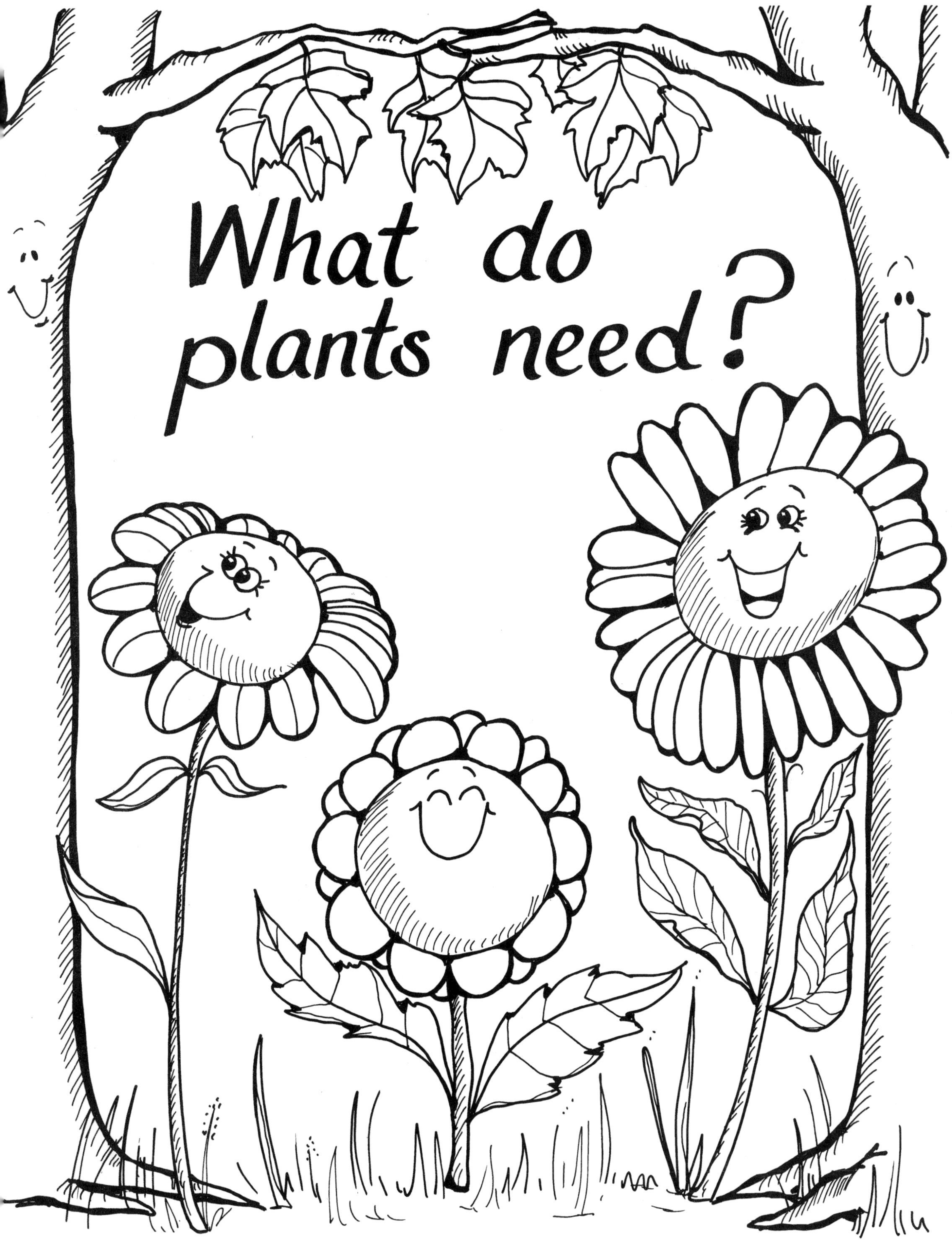
What do
plants need?

Plants need soil.

Plants need soil and water.

Plants need soil, water, and light.

Plants need soil, water, light, and space to grow.

People need plants for food.

People need plants for clothing.

People need plants for shelter.

I. **Topic Area**
Biological Science: Plants—People need plants

II. **Introductory Statement**
People use and enjoy many products from plants.

III. **Math Skills**
a. Graphing

Science Processes
a. Observation

IV. **Materials**
Vegetables
Wood
Flowers
Paper
Maple sugar
Cotton cloth
Pictures of trees
Cotton plants, corn plants

V. **Key Question**
Why are plants important to people?

VI. **Background Information**
People need plants to give oxygen and food. When plants make their food, they take in carbon dioxide and give off oxygen.
Plants are very important to people, as all food eaten comes directly or indirectly from plants.
People use plants for many other purposes. Clothing, medicines, lumber, paper and beauty all come from plants.

VII. **Management Suggestions**
1. Get as many examples of things that come from plants that people use as possible, such as paper, cotton, maple sugar, pencils, etc.
2. Use pictures of other places that plant products are used, such as construction, clothing, furniture, etc.

VIII. **Procedure**
1. Display pictures of trees in a forest, cotton plants ready to harvest, corn plants in a field. Discuss how these plants are used by humans.
2. Make a bulletin board labeled—Homes, Clothing, Food, Beauty, and Things We Use. Have the students cut out pictures of things that come from plants and place under the correct heading. Or use the actual examples of plants and their finished products. For example: wood-paper, pencil, cotton balls, pieces of cotton fabric, etc.

3. How many children have on cotton today? Have them stand and make a real world graph.
4. Look around the room, have students find objects that came from a plant. Discuss.

5. Discuss with the students what they had to eat for breakfast and what plants those foods came from.
6. Help the students understand the importance of plants by making a list of all the things we would lack if there were no plants.

IX. **Discussion**
1. What would happen if we did not have plants and plant products to use?
2. What would happen if all the flowers, trees, and beautiful plants disappeared?
3. Name some of the ways that plants are used for enjoyment.

X. **Extension**
1. Make a collage of things that come from plants: seeds, leaves, stems, cotton, etc.
2. Make sniff pictures from herbs. Children glue the herbs to a drawing, then share their fragrant picture with friends.
3. Make brightly colored leaf rubbings.
4. Write a thank-you letter to a plant.

My Name. ______________________

People Need Plants

Think of all the ways we use plants. Look around the room. Make a list.

1. ______________________
2. ______________________
3. ______________________
4. ______________________
5. ______________________
6. ______________________
7. ______________________
8. ______________________
9. ______________________
10. ______________________
11. ______________________
12. ______________________
13. ______________________
14. ______________________
15. ______________________
16. ______________________
17. ______________________
18. ______________________
19. ______________________
20. ______________________
21. ______________________
22. ______________________
23. ______________________
24. ______________________
25. ______________________
26. ______________________

Plant Parts

Each part of a plant has an important function.

Leaves are the parts of the plant where food is made by photosynthesis. Leaves take in carbon dioxide from the air, water from the soil, and energy from sunlight. During photosynthesis, the leaves use light energy to change carbon dioxide and water into sugars (food).

Flowers are the reproductive parts of a plant. Flower petals and the flower's smell attract bees and insects to pollinate the flower. After pollination, the petals fall away and seeds develop in the part of a flower called the ovary. The ovary itself usually becomes what we call fruit.

Stems support the upper parts of plants. Water and dissolved nutrients from the soil travel up the stem in a system of tubes. Food from the leaves travel down the stems to the roots. Stems also store food.

Roots of plants anchor the plants in the soil. Water and minerals are taken from the soil through the roots. Many plants such as carrots, store food in their roots.

Seeds contain a tiny embryo of a plant inside. The seed halves contain food which supplies energy and materials for growth until the plant grows its first leaves above the ground.

Observe a Leaf

I. Topic Area
Biological Science: Plant Parts—Leaves

II. Introductory Statement
Students will observe and describe leaves.

III. Math Skills
a. Measurement
b. Counting

Science Processes
a. Observation
b. Comparison

IV. Materials
Leaves—preferably those chosen by the children
Magnifying lens

V. Key Question
What does a leaf look like?

VI. Background Information

The variety to be found among the leaves of plants is enormous. There are large leaves, small leaves, slender leaves and wide ones. Leaves can be soft, prickly, hairy and hard.

But leaves all have one thing in common, they change sunlight into energy through photosynthesis. The leaves absorb carbon dioxide from the air and, with water that comes through the roots of the plant, combines these elements and releases oxygen into the air. By this exchange, plants maintain a level of oxygen in the air that benefits all living things.

VII. Management Suggestions
1. If possible, take the class on a nature hike and let the students pick up a special leaf of their own.
2. If a nature hike is not possible, have the students bring a leaf to study from home.
3. Don't let the leaves dry out; they will be hard for the students to work with when they are brittle.

VIII. Procedure
1. Tell the students to take their special leaf and look at it carefully. Draw it in the box on the worksheet.
2. Use a magnifying lens to look at the veins of the leaf.
3. Measure the length and width of the leaf.
4. Describe the leaf by filling in the blanks on the next page.
5. Take the leaf and trace around it on the graph paper.
6. Color the leaf you traced on the paper to look like your special leaf.

IX. Discussion Questions
1. Why do plants have leaves?
2. Do all leaves look alike?
3. Are all leaves green?
4. What do leaves do for a plant?
5. Do leaves ever change color?
6. What happens to deciduous leaves in the fall?

X. Extensions
1. Make a collection of as many different kinds of leaves as you can find.
2. Find some way to group the leaves.
3. Use the students' leaves to make leaf prints or leaf rubbings.
4. Arrange leaves on contact paper or waxed paper and place in a construction paper frame. Display in the window.
5. If this lesson cannot be done when the leaves are collected, keep them soft by putting them in a solution of 1 part glycerine to two parts water. Layer the leaves in a shallow pan, cover with the glycerine solution, soak for 24 hours. Remove and press between newspapers for 3 days. The colors will not be as bright as they were when they were collected, but the leaves will be soft and pliable.

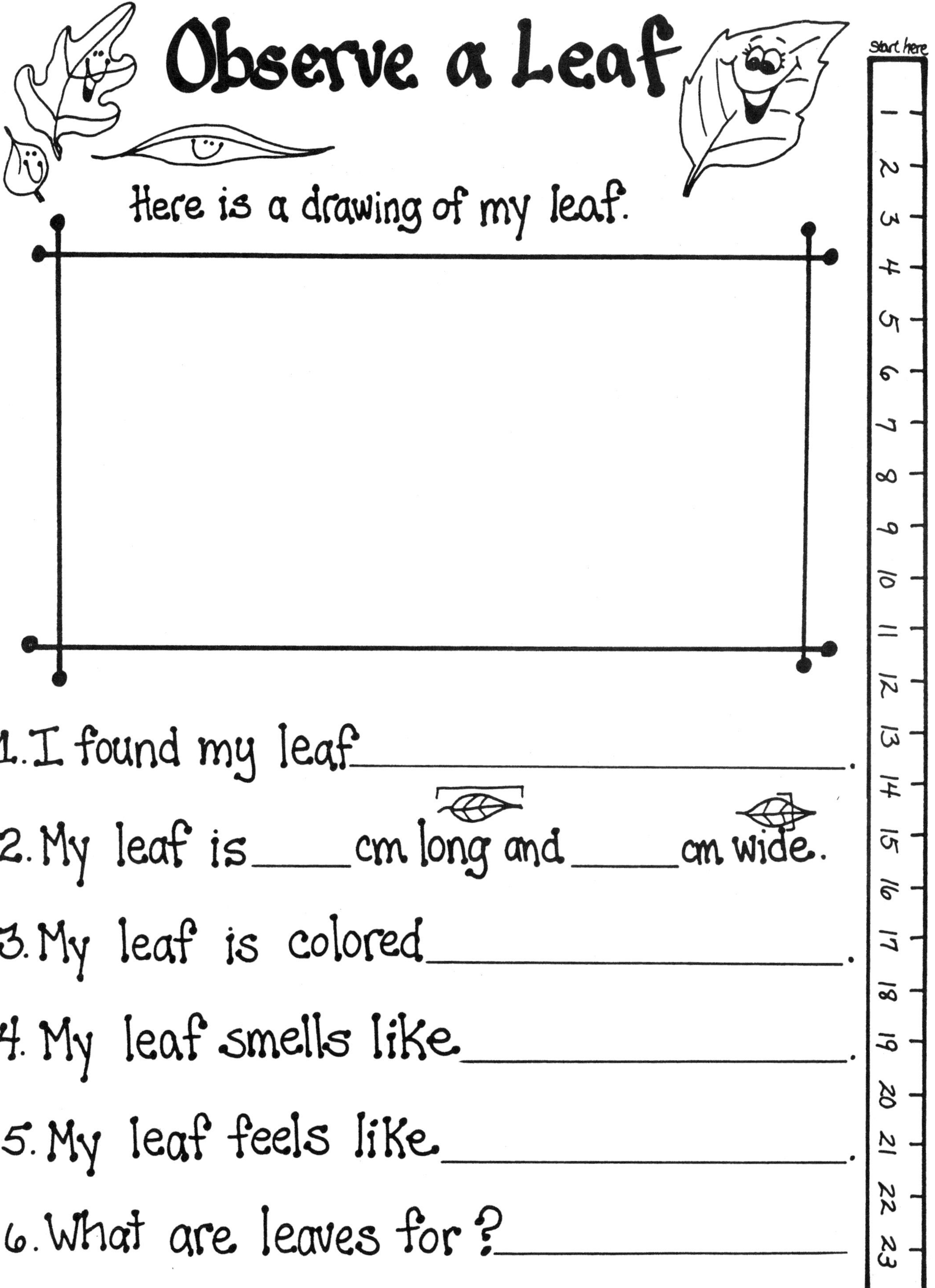

Observe a Leaf

Here is a drawing of my leaf.

1. I found my leaf ____________________.
2. My leaf is _____ cm long and _____ cm wide.
3. My leaf is colored ____________________.
4. My leaf smells like ____________________.
5. My leaf feels like ____________________.
6. What are leaves for? ____________________

Leafy Facts

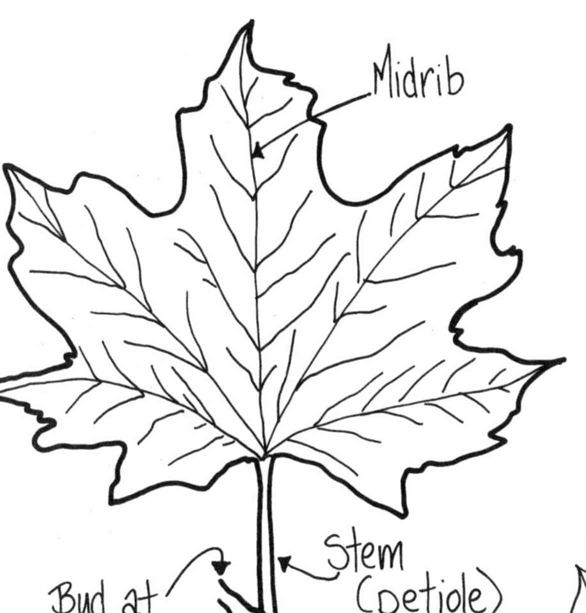

Simple Leaf

The broad, flat part of a leaf is called the blade. The blade is connected to the stem or petiole. The stem supports the blade and turns it towards the sun. The bud grows at the base of the leaf. The midrib is the central stalk of the leaf.

Compound Leaf

In some plants, the blades are divided into a number of small leaves called leaflets. A compound leaf has a number of leaves arranged in two rows facing each other along the midrib. One leaflet may grow at the tip of the midrib of some compound leaves. Buds always appear at the base of the leaf, never at the base of the leaflets.

More Leafy Facts

A blade of grass, a pine needle, a fern frond, and a maple leaf are all leaves. Most leaves need light, air, and water. Leaves contain green cells to make food for the entire plant.

Leaves look very different, however. Every plant has its own distinctive kind of leaf. Leaves help us identify plants like fingerprints identify people.

Needle like leaves can be divided into two groups. Needles can be attached singley to a stem. Other needlelike leaves have needles attached in bundles of two, three, and four.

Almost all other leaves can be grouped into broad leaves. Broad leaves can be further classified by their pattern of veins.

In palms, grasses, and other plants, the veins run parallel to one another from the petiole to blade tip.

The branched or webbed group can be classified into 2 groups– pinnate (featherlike) or palmate (fanlike.

In the pinnate group, the veins branch out from the midrib like barbs of a feather.

The veins in a palmate leaf fan out from the petiole and form a network of smaller veins through the leaf.

Leaf Safari

I. Topic Area
Biological Science—Plant Parts—Leaves

II. Introductory Statement
Students will compare, measure, and describe leaves.

III. Math Skills
a. Counting
b. Comparing
c. Measuring

Science Processes
a. Observing
b. Identifying
c. Recording

IV. Materials
A variety of leaves
Leaf collecting bag

V. Key Question
How are leaves different?

VI. Background Information

Green plants are the only living things that make their own food. Scientists call this process photosynthesis which means "making use of light". Green leaves contain a substance called chlorophyll which turns the light energy from the sun into food energy for the plant. Leaves take carbon dioxide from the air and water and convert them into glucose, oxygen and water. The glucose or simple sugar is carried to other parts of the plant through the veins in the leaves. The oxygen is released into the air through tiny pores or openings in the leaf called stomata. Leaves need sunlight in order to retain chlorophyll and produce food. All animal life depends on plants for food.

There is great variety in the shape, margins, surface and texture of leaves. A leaf is simple when it has one blade on one leaf stalk. It is compound when the blade is composed of several separate leaflets on one leaf stalk. The leaf may be long and narrow with the veins running parallel to the edge of the leaf. In others the veins branch out like a fan from the base of the leaf. This is called a palmate leaf. In the pinnate leaf, the veins are borne on the midrib and branch out along its length. The margins or edges of a leaf may be smooth, with sharp teeth, or deeply cut into fairly large portions, called lobes. The surface and texture of a leaf may be smooth or rough, or harsh to the touch.

VII. Management Suggestions
1. It is important for the class to go outside and collect leaves for the Leaf Safari.
2. Encourage the students to get as many different kinds of leaves as possible.

VIII. Procedure
1. Give each student a leaf collecting bag. Take the class outside for a guided leaf safari. Tell them to collect a variety of leaves and bring them back to the classroom. Complete the first Leaf Safari worksheet.
2. Discuss the likenesses and differences among the leaves collected. Use large loops of colored yarn to group the leaves into sets. Groupings could include long and thin, broad and flat, needlelike, jagged edges, shiny or dull, rough or smooth, or color, etc.
3. Make a language experience chart with descriptive words generated by the children.
4. Choose two attributes—large and shiny for example. Make the Venn diagram using the loops of yarn and place all the leaves in the proper set. Have the students take turns naming the sets and placing the leaves in the proper set. Describe each set by attribute and number in the set.
5. Observe leaves under a hand lens or magnifying glass. Identify the veins in the leaves and notice their shapes. Discuss the idea that these veins carry food, water and minerals to all parts of the leaf. Compare that idea to the veins in their own hands and arms and their similar function of carrying blood to parts of the body.
6. Use rulers to measure the lengths of 5-6 different leaves. Sequence the leaves in order from longest to shortest. Make a leaf rubbing on a long piece of paper to record this pattern.
7. Trace the leaves onto the graph paper. Count and number the squares to find the surface area. Order the leaves again to form a pattern of leaves from smallest in area to largest in area.

IX. Discussion
1. What three things do plants need to make their own food? (sunlight + chlorophyll + water = food)
2. How do leaves help the plant make food? (convert sunlight to food energy)
3. How are leaves alike? How are they different?

X. Extensions
1. Study types of leaves that we eat for food. Prepare vegetables for students to taste both raw and cooked. Let the students vote on which vegetable leaves they like and how they like them prepared. Edible leaves include kale, spinach, lettuce, parsley, collards, mustard greens and brussel sprouts.
2. Decorate a T-shirt with a leaf rubbing.
3. Write a Haiku poem or a two word poem about leaves.
4. Make a lasting collection of leaves by preserving them (see Observe a Leaf) and mounting them on a stiff piece of cardboard.

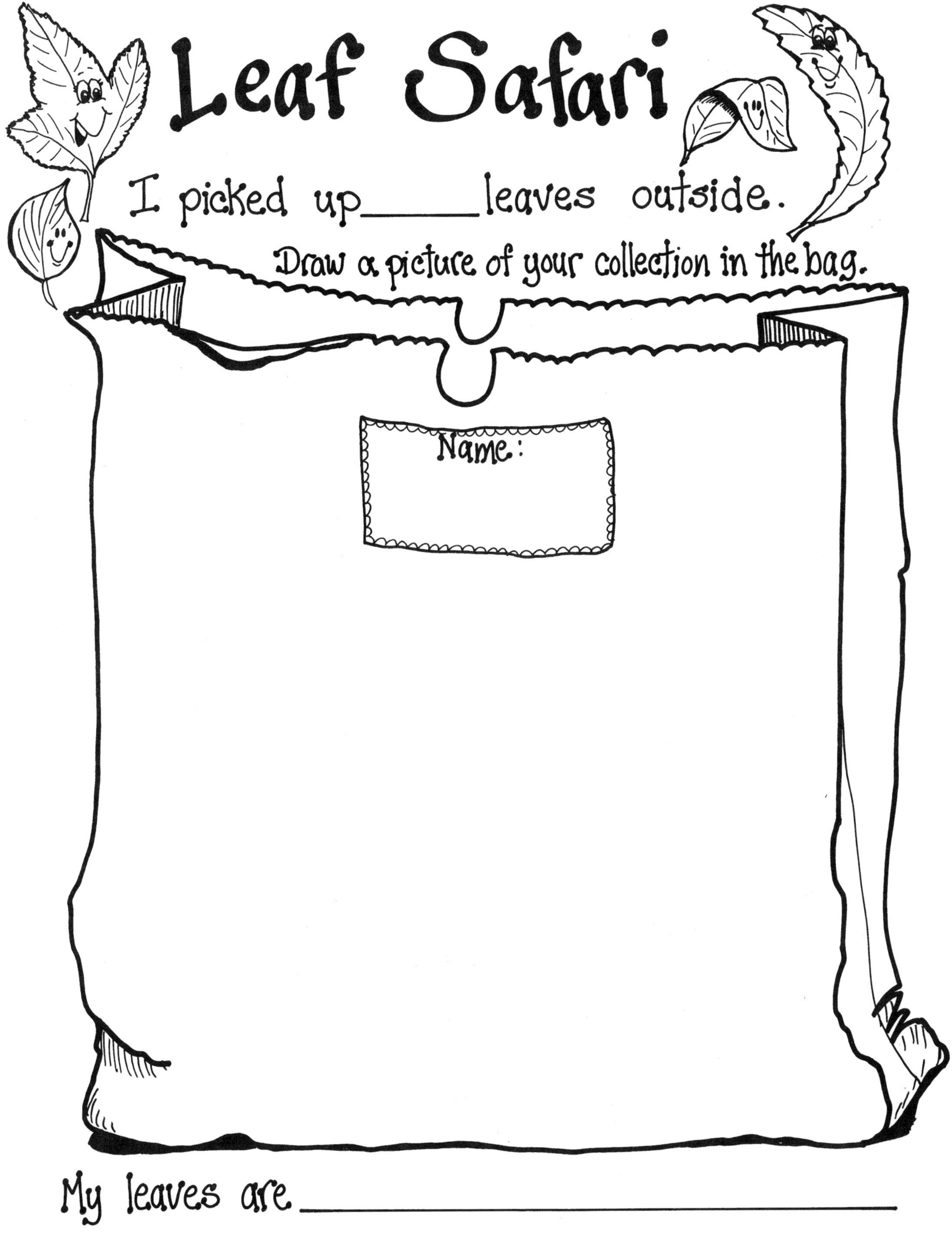

My leaves are____________________

________________________________.

Leaf Safari

My Name ____________

1. Pick your favorite leaf.

2. Describe the color and shape.

____

____

____

3. Trace your leaf on the grid.

4. Measure, count, and record:

Leaf length __________ Leaf width __________

Leaf area __________ squares

Stem Study

I. Topic Area
Biological Science: Plant Parts—Stems

II. Introductory Statement
Students will learn how stems are necessary to plants.

III. Math Skills
a. Comparing
b. Counting

Science Processes
a. Observing
b. Recording
c. Predicting

IV. Materials
Plants with different kinds of stems—celery, potato, asparagus
A celery stalk or daisy flower with stem
Food coloring
Plastic glasses

V. Key Question
What are the functions of a plant stem?

VI. Background Information

Stems of plants serve many functions. One function is to support the other plant parts that are above the ground. The stem holds up the plant's parts toward the sun so the plant can receive the light energy it needs. Some plants have stems that are soft and green. Others have stems that are thick and hard, like trees.

The most important function of a stem is to serve as a transport system in plants. Small tubes from the roots go up through the stems. Water and minerals are carried from the roots to the leaves of a plant. Food made in the leaves moves through the tubes in the stem to other parts of the plants.

Some stems are specialized organs used to store food. Stem vegetables include celery, asparagus, sugar cane, broccoli, and potatoes.

VII. Management Suggestions
1. Collect stems that are familiar to students as food they eat, such as celery, broccoli, asparagus, rhubarb, and potatoes.
2. Explain to the students that a potato is an underground stem, not a root.

VIII. Procedure
1. Take the students outside to identify plants and look at the stems of plants. Discuss and compare how plant stems are alike and different.
2. Discuss the functions of stems. Stems hold up other plant parts that are above the ground.

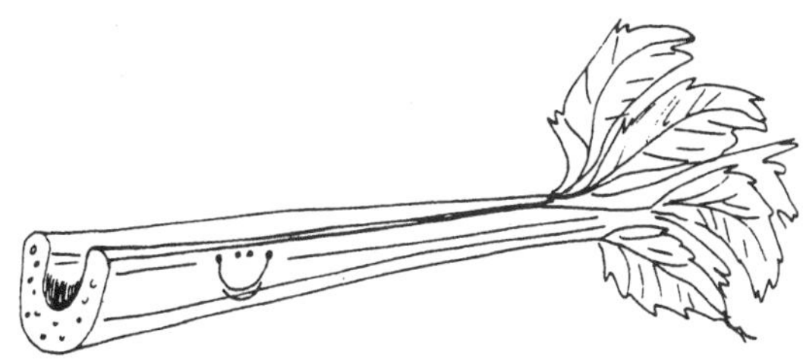

Stems also carry food and water from the roots, through the stems and into the leaves. Look at different stems of plants. Tree trunks are hard, thick stems. Flowers have soft, thin stems.
3. Discuss what stems we eat as vegetables—celery, broccoli, asparagus, rhubarb, sugar cane, and potatoes.
4. The worksheet "I Study a Stem" is a classic experiment but one that shows how a stem carries water to the leaves. Provide enough stalks of celery so that each child has one to draw. Ask the students to describe their celery stalk. List their descriptions on a giant celery shaped chart. Read through the experiment and ask for predictions to be made.

   Place the stalks in different colored water for variety. When the color has traveled all the way to the leaves, let the children cut the stalks apart to see the inside tubes.
5. Set up the "Flower in Water" experiment for the class; let them predict what they think will happen to the flower. Leave the flower in the glass overnight; have the students record what happened by drawing the flower on the worksheet.
6. As an extension to the "Flower in Water" do the "Colorful Changes". Fill three glasses with water. Color one blue, one red, and in the third, mix red and blue to make purple. Put one white flower (daisy, or carnation) into each glass. Have the students predict what will happen to each one. Most students will predict that the flowers will turn blue, red, and purple. What actually happens is sometimes surprising. The blue color will rise, the red color will rise, but the mixed purple often will separate back into red and blue as it rises.

IX. Discussion

1. How does the water and food travel through the stems into the leaves and flowers?
2. How are stems alike?
3. What differences do you see in stems?
4. Do all stems grow above ground?
5. Are all stems hard and thick like tree trunks?
6. Are all stems green? Name some that are not.

X. Extensions

1. Make rubbings of various kinds of stems. Rubbings can be made by placing a piece of paper over an object and then rubbing with the side of a crayon.
2. Discuss with the students what people use tree stems for. Discuss the lumber industry. Make a large tree trunk shaped chart; list all the uses we have for trees (furniture, houses, baseball bats, etc.).

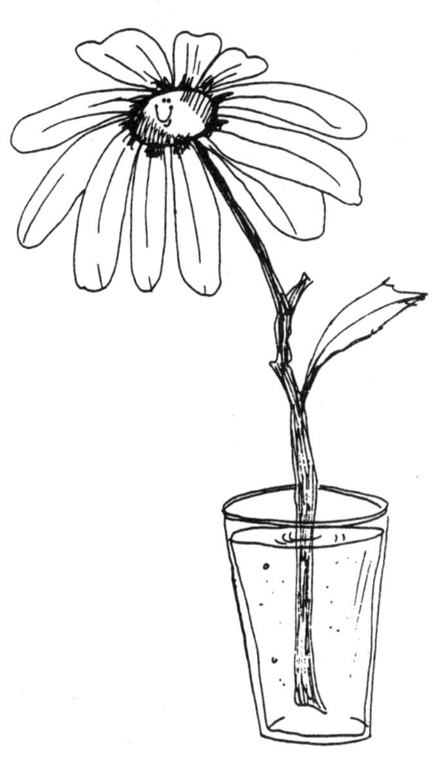

____
My Name

Stem Study

Here is a drawing of my stem.

My stem is from a ______________.

1. Put some water in a glass.
2. Add 4 drops of food coloring.
3. Cut off the end of the stem.
4. Place the stem in the glass.
5. Leave overnight.

What happened? ______________

____

Why? ______________________________

____

What are stems for? ______________________

Flower in Water

1. Pour water in a glass.
2. Color the water red.
3. Put a flower in the water.
4. Draw the flower.
5. Leave overnight.

6. How did the flower change? ______________________________

____

Colorful Changes

Name ____________________

1. Add food coloring to the cups.
2. Put a flower with stem in each cup.
3. Draw the three flowers. Color.
4. Leave the flowers overnight.

What do you think will happen?

1. Look at the flowers.
2. Draw the changes.

red
blue
red + blue

What really happened?

Super Tuber

I. Topic Area
Biological Science: Plant Parts—Tubers

II. Introductory Statement
Students will learn that potatoes are underground stems.

III. Math Skills
a. Counting
b. Weighing
c. Graphing

Science Processes
a. Observation
b. Recording Data
c. Comparing

IV. Materials
Sack of potatoes
Centimeter tape
Scales

V. Key Question
How different is a potato from other kinds of plant stems?

VI. Background Information

The potato, though it grows underground, is not a root of the plant, but a stem. The potato plant has stems, roots, leaves and flowers. But there are swellings on the underground parts of the stems. These swellings are called "tubers" and are what we call potatoes.

Look carefully at a potato. The "eyes" on a potato are tiny buds with a small scale-like leaf beside each eye. If you cut an eye from a potato and plant it in the soil, the bud will grow a new plant.

Potatoes are a basic food for millions of people throughout the world. The potato was first grown in South America and spread from there to Europe and North America by Spanish travelers.

VII. Management Suggestion
1. Bring in enough potatoes for each student to have one.

VIII. Procedure
1. Bring in a sack of potatoes hidden in a grocery bag. Pass the bag around and let the students feel the bag and predict what they think is inside.
2. Play a quick game of 20 questions. Students may ask questions and you may answer with only yes or no. When someone guesses correctly, bring the potatoes out of the bag to show.
3. Explain that a potato is an underground stem, not a root. A potato plant has roots, stems, leaves and flowers, but there are swellings on the underground parts of the stems of the plant. These swellings are called tubers and we call these tubers potatoes.

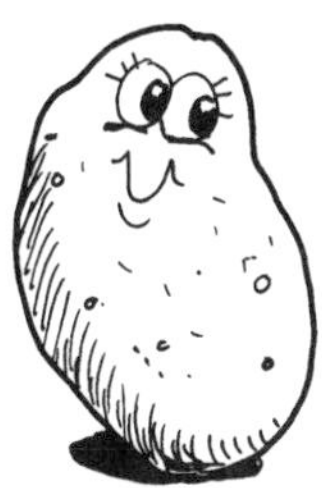

4. Give each child a tuber to study. Have them draw and color, count the number of eyes, measure, weigh and record the information about their potato.
5. Gather the class information on a chart or on one of the graphs included in this lesson.
6. After the class makes a bar graph of how they like potatoes, make a large Venn diagram from 3 or more of the choices and allow them to post their preference with colored round stickers or small pieces of paper. Use one color for girls and a different color for boys. Discuss the results of the survey as a math lesson.

IX. Discussion
1. How many eyes are there on a potato?
2. What will grow from the eye of a potato?
3. What are potatoes used for?
4. What is a tuber?
5. Where are the leaves and flowers of a potato plant?
6. If a potato is an underground stem, where are the roots of the plant?

X. Extensions
1. Make potato prints.
2. Leave a potato in a dark closet for several weeks. What happens to it?
3. If you have space, plant an eye of the potato and let the students see where the potatoes grow.

______________ My name

Super Tuber

1. Here is a picture of my tuber.
2. My tuber is called a ______________.

Count and Measure

3. My potato has _______ eyes.
4. My potato is ______ cm long.
5. My potato weighs ______ teddy bears.
6. I like to eat my potatoes ____________.

raw	mashed	fried	baked	boiled

How do you like your potatoes?

Root Study

I. Topic Area
Biological Science: Plant Parts—Roots

II. Introductory Statement
The students will be able to describe the functions of the roots of a plant.

III. Math Skills
a. Measuring
b. Graphing

Science Processes
a. Observation
b. Comparing

IV. Materials
Several plants with different root systems: dandelion, grass, carrot, radish, sweet potato
Magnifying lens

V. Key Question
Why do plants need roots? Do all root systems look alike?

VI. Background Information

Plant root systems are very essential to plants. The function of the roots is to anchor plants and absorb water and nutrients from the surrounding soil.

Plant root systems may vary in several ways. Taproots are large central roots that grow deep into the soil. Smaller roots extend from this central root. A carrot root is an example of a taproot.

Fibrous roots obtain more surface water. They are shallow roots that spread over a wide area. Fibrous roots branch considerably and have a threadlike appearance. Grass roots are fibrous roots.

When a seed begins to grow, the roots always grow first. Gravity causes the roots to grow down towards the earth and the stem up towards the sun.

VII. Management Suggestion
Obtain several examples of fibrous roots and taproots. Be sure the students know there are two different kinds of root systems.

VIII. Procedure
1. Wash the soil from the roots of several plants and display them: grass, dandelion, radish, carrot. Have the students use a magnifying lens to observe these roots. Introduce the terms tap and fibrous for the roots. Taproots have several individual roots that branch out. Discuss how roots absorb water. Tell the students that water moves through the roots to the plant.
2. Do the student page, "I Study a Root". Provide a variety of roots. Let the children pick one of the roots to study. They must write its name, draw its picture, describe where it is found, measure its length, and write one sentence about it. Sample roots include radish, onion, carrot, turnip, grass, or sweet potato.
3. Grow a plant from a sweet potato (a root). Place the potato in a clean glass with water. Place it in a sunny window and watch it grow. Measure the growth of the plant daily. Chart, graph, or illustrate the plant's growth.

IX. Discussion
1. Why does a plant need roots?
2. Do roots all look alike?
3. Are roots all the same color?
4. Would a tree have a taproot or fibrous roots?
5. Why would a tree need a deep taproot while grass or weeds don't?
6. Explain the difference between plants with fibrous roots and those with taproots.

X. Extension
1. Write a story about a root's search for water and food.

My name.: ______________________

Root Study

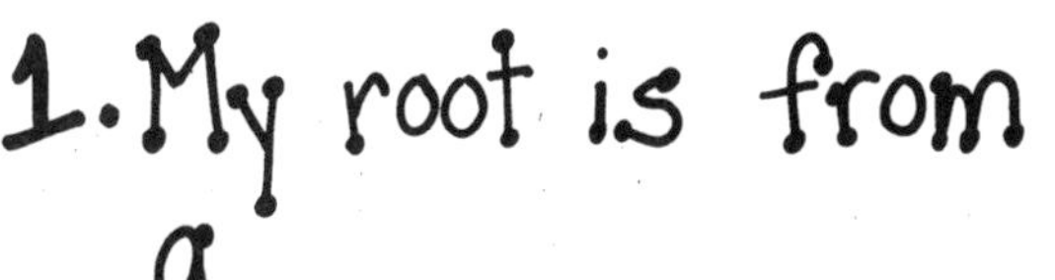

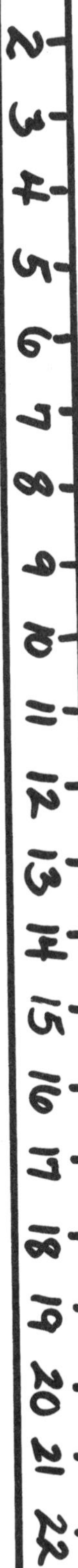

Here is a drawing of my root.

1. My root is from a ______________________.

2. My root is colored ______________________ ______________________.

3. My root is ______ cm long and ______ cm wide.

4. I ______________ eat this root.
   (could, could not)

5. What are roots for? ______________________ ______________________ ______________________

Flowers

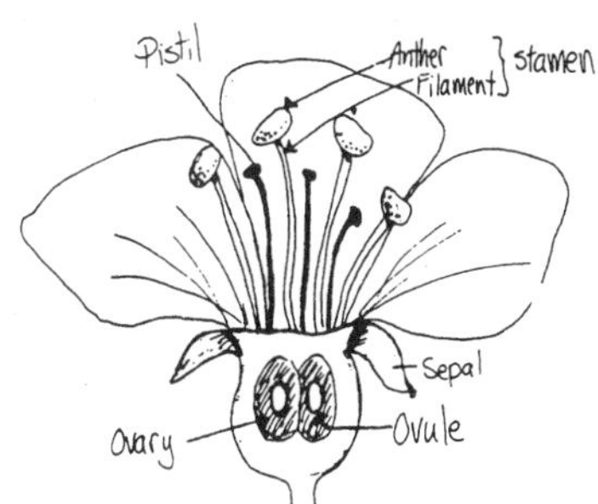

I. Topic Area
Biological Science: Plant Parts—Flowers

II. Introductory Statement
The student will describe the parts of a flower.

III. Math Skills
a. Counting
b. Graphing

Science Processes
a. Observation
b. Comparing

IV. Materials
1 flower per student
Magnifying lenses
1 8 × 10 piece of contact paper per student
Crayons
Butcher paper for graphing

V. Key Question
What is the function of a flower?

VI. Background Information

A flower's function is to make seeds to reproduce the plant. The flower contains the reproductive parts of a flowering plant. Petals are not just to be pretty, they actually attract birds, bees, and other insects to the flower so that pollenation can occur. When pollen from the stamen (male) lands on the stigma (female) a long pollen tube grows down the stalk of the pistil into the ovary.

When ovules inside of the ovary are fertilized by a pollen grain, it can develop into a seed. The ovary then develops into a fruit which protects the seeds.

VII. Management Suggestion
1. Use a flower like a daisy whose parts are easy to separate and observe. Don't use a flower with too many petals.

VIII. Procedure
1. Bring enough flowers to class so that each child can have one. Daisies work well.
2. Have the students study their flower with a hand lens and record their findings on the sheet "This Is My Flower". Have them draw their flower in the frame, then take their flowers apart and observe with the hand lens.
3. After they take their flowers apart, give them a small piece of contact paper in the shape of a rectangle. let them arrange the flower's parts into a design on one half of the paper. Fold the half over to make a sandwich. Place in a construction paper frame and display in the window.

4. Make a large wall graph. To post results on the graph, use the flower patterns or have the children draw their own flower on a post-it square and stick it to the chart. Use the information gathered about number of petals.

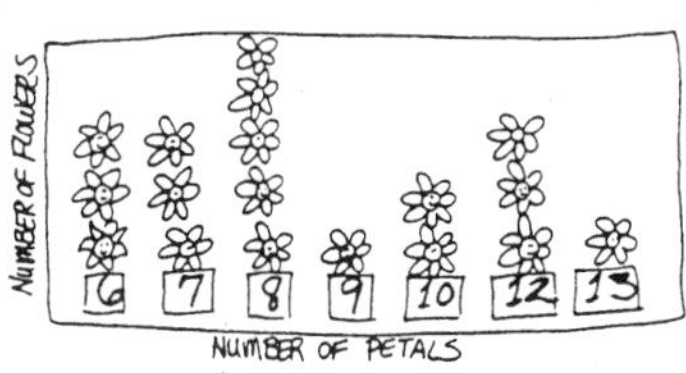

5. On another day, ask the children to bring flowers from home. Describe and compare the flowers that come in. Make a graph of the colors or let the children vote on their favorite color of flower.

IX. Discussion
1. Are flowers mainly of just one color?
2. How do you think bees and butterflies find the flowers?
3. Why are flowers usually not black, brown or green?
4. Do bright colors make flowers more attractive to bees, birds, and butterflies?
5. What number of petals occurs most frequently on the flowers studied?
6. What is the favorite color of flower for the class?

X. Extension
1. Do a study on bees. Discuss how flowers attract bees. Explain how bees carry pollen to other flowers and what bees do with the pollen.
2. Use flowers as models for art work. Students can do their favorite flower in watercolor, crayon resist, chalk, torn construction paper, or a tissue paper collage.
3. Write two word poetry about flowers:

   My flower,
   Looks soft,
   Smells sweet,
   Grows tall,
   Tickles me.
4. Complete the sentence: Flowers are like ____ ________________. Illustrate and display.
5. Brainstorm all the words that begin with the letter F to describe flowers: (fancy, flat, floppy, flashy, fair, foul, fuzzy, funny flowers)

This is My Flower

______________________ My Name

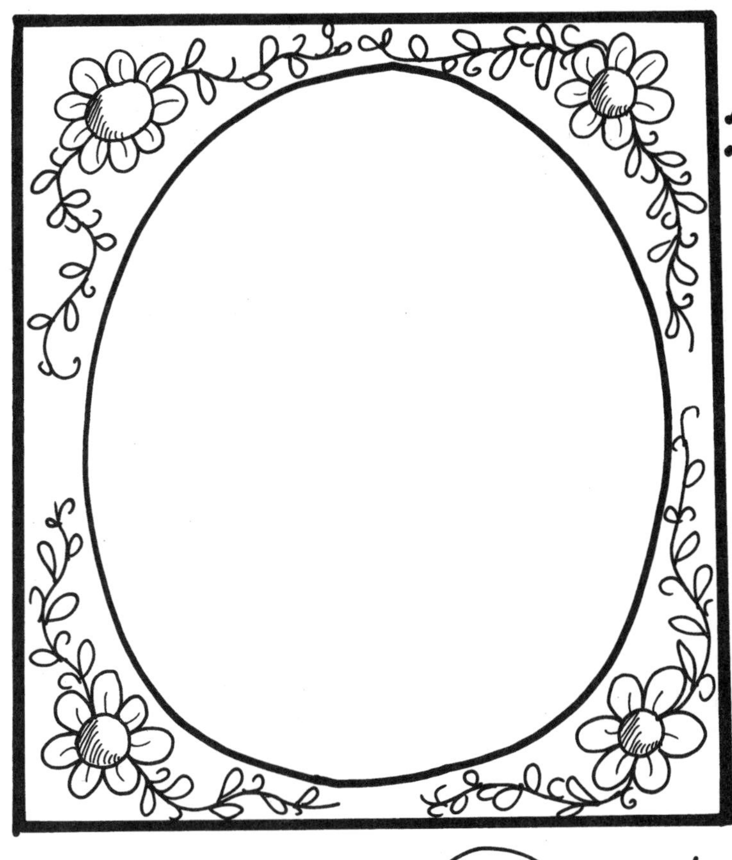

1. The colors in my flower are ______________________ ______________________.

2. My flower has ________ petals.

3. My flower smells like ______________________.

4. Make a pollen print.

5. What are flowers for? ______________________

____

____

Glossary

Algae–a small plant that does not have roots, stems, leaves or flowers, but makes its own food

Bulb–a large bud that is planted and which grows to form roots, leaves and flowers

Carbon Dioxide–a gas in the air that is used by plants to make their food

Chlorophyll–the green colored substance in plants that absorbs energy from sunlight

Cotyledon–a seed leaf

Deciduous–a kind of tree that loses its leaves every autumn

Dicot–a plant whose seeds have two sections

Embryo–the tiny plant within a seed

Flower–a part of the plant that is colorful and makes seeds

Fern–a group of non seed bearing plants that have roots, stems and leaves

Fibrous Roots–shallow roots that grow over a wide area

Frond–a fern leaf that grows upward from the stem

Fruit–the part of a plant that holds the seeds

Germinate–when a seed starts to grow and produces a new plant

Leaf–the flat, thin part of a plant that grows on the stem

Monocot–a plant whose seeds have one section

Ovary–bottom, rounded part of a pistil in which the ovules are located

Ovule–the female reproductive part of a plant that contains an egg

Petal–a part of a flower that often is brightly colored

Photosynthesis–the process in which green plants use carbon dioxide, water and energy from sunlight to make their own food.

Pistil–female organ of a flower

Pollination–transfer of pollen from the stamens to the pistils of flowers

Seed–the small object within a fruit that will grow into a new plant

Seed Coat–the tough outside part found on many seeds

Spores–the cells in non seed plants used to reproduce

Stamen–the part of the flower that makes the yellow dust-like powder

Stigma–the very top of the pistil

Tap Root–large central roots that grow deep into the soil

Tuber–the underground stem of a plant, where starch is stored

The AIMS Program

AIMS is the acronym for "**A**ctivities **I**ntegrating **M**athematics and **S**cience." Such integration enriches learning and makes it meaningful and holistic. AIMS began as a project of Fresno Pacific University to integrate the study of mathematics and science in grades K-9, but has since expanded to include language arts, social studies, and other disciplines.

AIMS is a continuing program of the non-profit AIMS Education Foundation. It had its inception in a National Science Foundation funded program whose purpose was to explore the effectiveness of integrating mathematics and science. The project directors in cooperation with 80 elementary classroom teachers devoted two years to a thorough field-testing of the results and implications of integration.

The approach met with such positive results that the decision was made to launch a program to create instructional materials incorporating this concept. Despite the fact that thoughtful educators have long recommended an integrative approach, very little appropriate material was available in 1981 when the project began. A series of writing projects have ensued and today the AIMS Education Foundation is committed to continue the creation of new integrated activities on a permanent basis.

The AIMS program is funded through the sale of this developing series of books and proceeds from the Foundation's endowment. All net income from program and products flows into a trust fund administered by the AIMS Education Foundation. Use of these funds is restricted to support of research, development, and publication of new materials. Writers donate all their rights to the Foundation to support its on-going program. No royalties are paid to the writers.

The rationale for integration lies in the fact that science, mathematics, language arts, social studies, etc., are integrally interwoven in the real world from which it follows that they should be similarly treated in the classroom where we are preparing students to live in that world. Teachers who use the AIMS program give enthusiastic endorsement to the effectiveness of this approach.

Science encompasses the art of questioning, investigating, hypothesizing, discovering, and communicating. Mathematics is a language that provides clarity, objectivity, and understanding. The language arts provide us powerful tools of communication. Many of the major contemporary societal issues stem from advancements in science and must be studied in the context of the social sciences. Therefore, it is timely that all of us take seriously a more holistic mode of educating our students. This goal motivates all who are associated with the AIMS Program. We invite you to join us in this effort.

Meaningful integration of knowledge is a major recommendation coming from the nation's professional science and mathematics associations. The American Association for the Advancement of Science in *Science for All Americans* strongly recommends the integration of mathematics, science, and technology. The National Council of Teachers of Mathematics places strong emphasis on applications of mathematics such as are found in science investigations. AIMS is fully aligned with these recommendations.

Extensive field testing of AIMS investigations confirms these beneficial results.

1. Mathematics becomes more meaningful, hence more useful, when it is applied to situations that interest students.
2. The extent to which science is studied and understood is increased, with a significant economy of time, when mathematics and science are integrated.
3. There is improved quality of learning and retention, supporting the thesis that learning which is meaningful and relevant is more effective.
4. Motivation and involvement are increased dramatically as students investigate real-world situations and participate actively in the process.

We invite you to become part of this classroom teacher movement by using an integrated approach to learning and sharing any suggestions you may have. The AIMS Program welcomes you!

AIMS Education Foundation Programs

A Day with AIMS®

Intensive one-day workshops are offered to introduce educators to the philosophy and rationale of AIMS. Participants will discuss the methodology of AIMS and the strategies by which AIMS principles may be incorporated into curriculum. Each participant will take part in a variety of hands-on AIMS investigations to gain an understanding of such aspects as the scientific/mathematical content, classroom management, and connections with other curricular areas. *A Day with AIMS®* workshops may be offered anywhere in the United States. Necessary supplies and take-home materials are usually included in the enrollment fee.

A Week with AIMS®

Throughout the nation, AIMS offers many one-week workshops each year, usually in the summer. Each workshop lasts five days and includes at least 30 hours of AIMS hands-on instruction. Participants are grouped according to the grade level(s) in which they are interested. Instructors are members of the AIMS Instructional Leadership Network. Supplies for the activities and a generous supply of take-home materials are included in the enrollment fee. Sites are selected on the basis of applications submitted by educational organizations. If chosen to host a workshop, the host agency agrees to provide specified facilities and cooperate in the promotion of the workshop. The AIMS Education Foundation supplies workshop materials as well as the travel, housing, and meals for instructors.

AIMS One-Week Perspectives Workshops

Each summer, Fresno Pacific University offers AIMS one-week workshops on its campus in Fresno, California. AIMS Program Directors and highly qualified members of the AIMS National Leadership Network serve as instructors.

The AIMS Instructional Leadership Program

This is an AIMS staff-development program seeking to prepare facilitators for leadership roles in science/math education in their home districts or regions. Upon successful completion of the program, trained facilitators may become members of the AIMS Instructional Leadership Network, qualified to conduct AIMS workshops, teach AIMS in-service courses for college credit, and serve as AIMS consultants. Intensive training is provided in mathematics, science, process and thinking skills, workshop management, and other relevant topics.

College Credit and Grants

Those who participate in workshops may often qualify for college credit. If the workshop takes place on the campus of Fresno Pacific University, that institution may grant appropriate credit. If the workshop takes place off-campus, arrangements can sometimes be made for credit to be granted by another institution. In addition, the applicant's home school district is often willing to grant in-service or professional-development credit. Many educators who participate in AIMS workshops are recipients of various types of educational grants, either local or national. Nationally known foundations and funding agencies have long recognized the value of AIMS mathematics and science workshops to educators. The AIMS Education Foundation encourages educators interested in attending or hosting workshops to explore the possibilities suggested above. Although the Foundation strongly supports such interest, it reminds applicants that they have the primary responsibility for fulfilling *current* requirements.

For current information regarding the programs described above, please complete the following:

Information Request

Please send current information on the items checked:

____ *Basic Information Packet* on AIMS materials
____ *AIMS Instructional Leadership Program*
____ *AIMS One-Week Perspectives* workshops
____ *A Week with AIMS®* workshops
____ Hosting information for *A Day with AIMS®* workshops
____ Hosting information for *A Week with AIMS®* workshops

Name ____________________ Phone ____________________

Address ____
Street City State Zip

We invite you to subscribe to AIMS®!

Each issue of AIMS® contains a variety of material useful to educators at all grade levels. Feature articles of lasting value deal with topics such as mathematical or science concepts, curriculum, assessment, the teaching of process skills, and historical background. Several of the latest AIMS math/science investigations are always included, along with their reproducible activity sheets. As needs direct and space allows, various issues contain news of current developments, such as workshop schedules, activities of the AIMS Instructional Leadership Network, and announcements of upcoming publications.

AIMS® is published monthly, August through May. Subscriptions are on an annual basis only. A subscription entered at any time will begin with the next issue, but will also include the previous issues of that volume. Readers have preferred this arrangement because articles and activities within an annual volume are often interrelated.

Please note that an AIMS® subscription automatically includes duplication rights for one school site for all issues included in the subscription. Many schools build cost-effective library resources with their subscriptions.

YES! I am interested in subscribing to AIMS®.

Name ______________________ Home Phone ______________________

Address ______________________ City, State, Zip ______________________

Please send the following volumes (subject to availability):

______Volume	VIII	(1993-94)	$15.00	______Volume	XIII	(1998-99)	$30.00
______Volume	IX	(1994-95)	$15.00	______Volume	XIV	(1999-00)	$30.00
______Volume	X	(1995-96)	$15.00	______Volume	XV	(2000-01)	$30.00
______Volume	XI	(1996-97)	$30.00	______Volume	XVI	(2001-02)	$30.00
______Volume	XII	(1997-98)	$30.00	______Volume	XVII	(2002-03)	$30.00

______**Limited offer: Volumes XVII & XVIII (2002-2004) $55.00**
(Note: Prices may change without notice)

Check your method of payment:

❒ Check enclosed in the amount of $__________

❒ Purchase order attached (Please include the P.O.#, the authorizing signature, and position of the authorizing person.)

❒ Credit Card ❒ Visa ❒ MasterCard Amount $ ______________

Card # ______________________ Expiration Date ____________

Signature ______________________ Today's Date ____________

Make checks payable to **AIMS Education Foundation.**
Mail to AIMS® Magazine, P.O. Box 8120, Fresno, CA 93747-8120.
Phone (559) 255-4094 or (888) 733-2467 FAX (559) 255-6396
AIMS Homepage: http://www.AIMSedu.org/

AIMS Program Publications

Actions with Fractions 4-9
Awesome Addition and Super Subtraction 2-3
Bats Incredible! 2-4
Brick Layers 4-9
Brick Layers II 4-9
Counting on Coins 1-2
Crazy about Cotton Book 3-7
Critters K-6
Cycles of Knowing and Growing 1-3
Down to Earth 5-9
Electrical Connections 4-9
Exploring Environments Book K-6
Fabulous Fractions 3-6
Fall into Math and Science K-1
Field Detectives 3-6
Finding Your Bearings 4-9
Floaters and Sinkers 5-9
From Head to Toe 5-9
Fun with Foods 5-9
Glide into Winter with Math & Science K-1
Gravity Rules! Activity Book 5-12
Hardhatting in a Geo-World 3-5
It's About Time K-2
Jaw Breakers and Heart Thumpers 3-5
Just for the Fun of It! 4-9
Looking at Lines 6-9
Machine Shop 5-9
Magnificent Microworld Adventures 5-9
Marvelous Multiplication and Dazzling Division 4-5
Math + Science, A Solution 5-9
Mostly Magnets 2-8
Multiplication the Algebra Way 4-8
Off The Wall Science 3-9
Our Wonderful World 5-9
Out of This World 4-8
Overhead and Underfoot 3-5
Paper Square Geometry: The Mathematics of Origami
Puzzle Play: 4-8
Pieces and Patterns 5-9
Popping With Power 3-5
Primarily Bears K-6
Primarily Earth K-3
Primarily Physics K-3
Primarily Plants K-3
Proportional Reasoning 6-9
Ray's Reflections 4-8
Sense-Able Science K-1
Soap Films and Bubbles 4-9
Spatial Visualization 4-9
Spills and Ripples 5-12
Spring into Math and Science K-1
The Amazing Circle 4-9
The Budding Botanist 3-6
The Sky's the Limit 5-9
Through the Eyes of the Explorers 5-9
Under Construction K-2
Water Precious Water 2-6
Weather Sense: Moisture 4-5
Weather Sense: Temperature, Air Pressure, and Wind 4-5
Winter Wonders K-2

Spanish/English Editions

Brinca de alegria hacia la Primavera con las Matemáticas y Ciencias K-1
Cáete de gusto hacia el Otoño con las Matemáticas y Ciencias K-1
Conexiones Eléctricas 4-9
El Botanista Principiante 3-6
Los Cinco Sentidos K-1
Ositos Nada Más K-6
Patine al Invierno con Matemáticas y Ciencias K-1
Piezas y Diseños 5-9
Primariamente Física K-3
Primariamente Plantas K-3
Principalmente Imanes 2-8

All Spanish/English Editions include student pages in Spanish and teacher and student pages in English.

Spanish Edition
Constructores II: Ingeniería Creativa Con Construcciones LEGO® (4-9)
The entire book is written in Spanish. English pages not included.

Other Science and Math Publications
Historical Connections in Mathematics, Vol. I 5-9
Historical Connections in Mathematics, Vol. II 5-9
Historical Connections in Mathematics, Vol. III 5-9
Mathematicians are People, Too
Mathematicians are People, Too, Vol. II
Teaching Science with Everyday Things
What's Next, Volume 1, 4-12
What's Next, Volume 2, 4-12
What's Next, Volume 3, 4-12

For further information write to:
AIMS Education Foundation • P.O. Box 8120 • Fresno, California 93747-8120
www.AIMSedu.org/ • Fax 559•255•6396

AIMS Duplication Rights Program

AIMS has received many requests from school districts for the purchase of unlimited duplication rights to AIMS materials. In response, the AIMS Education Foundation has formulated the program outlined below. There is a built-in flexibility which, we trust, will provide for those who use AIMS materials extensively to purchase such rights for either individual activities or entire books.

It is the goal of the AIMS Education Foundation to make its materials and programs available at reasonable cost. All income from the sale of publications and duplication rights is used to support AIMS programs; hence, strict adherence to regulations governing duplication is essential. Duplication of AIMS materials beyond limits set by copyright laws and those specified below is strictly forbidden.

Limited Duplication Rights

Any purchaser of an AIMS book may make up to *200 copies* of any activity in that book for use at *one school site*. Beyond that, rights must be purchased according to the appropriate category.

Unlimited Duplication Rights for Single Activities

An individual or school may purchase the right to make an unlimited number of copies of a single activity. The royalty is $5.00 per activity per school site.

Examples: 3 activities x 1 site x $5.00 = $15.00
9 activities x 3 sites x $5.00 = $135.00

Unlimited Duplication Rights for Entire Books

A school or district may purchase the right to make an unlimited number of copies of a single, *specified* book. The royalty is $20.00 per book per school site. This is in addition to the cost of the book.

Examples: 5 books x 1 site x $20.00 = $100.00
12 books x 10 sites x $20.00 = $2400.00

Magazine/Newsletter Duplication Rights

Those who purchase *AIMS*® (magazine)/*Newsletter* are hereby granted permission to make up to 200 copies of any portion of it, provided these copies will be used for educational purposes.

Workshop Instructors' Duplication Rights

Workshop instructors may distribute to registered workshop participants a maximum of 100 copies of any article and/or 100 copies of no more than eight activities, provided these six conditions are met:

1. Since all AIMS activities are based upon the *AIMS Model of Mathematics* and the *AIMS Model of Learning*, leaders must include in their presentations an explanation of these two models.
2. Workshop instructors must relate the AIMS activities presented to these basic explanations of the AIMS philosophy of education.
3. The copyright notice must appear on all materials distributed.
4. Instructors must provide information enabling participants to order books and magazines from the Foundation.
5. Instructors must inform participants of their limited duplication rights as outlined below.
6. Only student pages may be duplicated.

Written permission must be obtained for duplication beyond the limits listed above. Additional royalty payments may be required.

Workshop Participants' Rights

Those enrolled in workshops in which AIMS student activity sheets are distributed may duplicate a maximum of 35 copies or enough to use the lessons one time with one class, whichever is less. Beyond that, rights must be purchased according to the appropriate category.

Application for Duplication Rights

The purchasing agency or individual must clearly specify the following:

1. Name, address, and telephone number
2. Titles of the books for Unlimited Duplication Rights contracts
3. Titles of activities for Unlimited Duplication Rights contracts
4. Names and addresses of school sites for which duplication rights are being purchased.

*NOTE: **Books to be duplicated must be purchased separately and are not included in the contract for Unlimited Duplication Rights.***

The requested duplication rights are automatically authorized when proper payment is received, although a *Certificate of Duplication Rights* will be issued when the application is processed.

Address all correspondence to: **Contract Division**
AIMS Education Foundation
P.O. Box 8120
Fresno, CA 93747-8120

www.AIMSedu.org/
Fax 559•255•6396